WHEN YOU PRAY

WHEN YOU PRAY

Making the Lord's Prayer Your Own

PHILIP GRAHAM RYKEN

WITH DISCUSSION QUESTIONS
BY NANCY RYKEN TAYLOR

CROSSWAY BOOKS • WHEATON, ILLINOIS
A DIVISION OF GOOD NEWS PUBLISHERS

When You Pray

Copyright © 2000 by Philip Graham Ryken

Published by Crossway Books
        a division of Good News Publishers
        1300 Crescent Street
        Wheaton, Illinois 60187

Cover design: Cindy Kiple

First printing 2000

Printed in the United States of America

Unless otherwise noted, Scripture is taken from the *Holy Bible: New International Version*®. Copyright © 1973, 1978, 1984 by International Bible Society. Used by permission of Zondervan Publishing House. All rights reserved.

The "NIV" and "New International Version" trademarks are registered in the United States Patent and Trademark Office by International Bible Society. Use of either trademark requires the permission of International Bible Society.

Scripture identified as KJV is taken from the King James Version of the Bible.

Library of Congress Cataloging-in-Publication Data

Ryken, Philip Graham, 1966-
  When you pray : making the Lord's prayer your own / Philip Graham
    p.   cm.
  Includes bibliographical references and index.
  ISBN 1-58134-194-6 (alk. paper)
  1. Lord's prayer—Criticism, interpretation, etc. 2. Spiritual life—
Christianity. I. Title.
BV230.R95 2000
226.9'606—dc21   00-009759
                                  CIP

15	14	13	12	11	10	09	08	07	06	05	04	03	02	01	00
15	14	13	12	11	10	9	8	7	6	5	4	3	2	1	

To Joshua Philip Ryken—
who brings joy to his father's heart,
and to our Father in heaven—
who has made us brothers in Christ forever

Contents

Preface

The Lord's Prayer is the most wonderful prayer in the world. One beautiful description of its many perfections comes from the pen of Dr. Adolph Saphir:

> It is a model prayer, and as such commends itself to the most superficial glance—approves itself at once to the conscience of man. It is beautiful and symmetrical, like the most finished work of art. The words are plain and unadorned, yet majestic; and so transparent and appropriate that, once fixed in the memory, no other expressions ever mix themselves up with them; the thought of substituting other words never enters the mind. Grave and solemn are the petitions, yet the serenity and tranquil confidence, the peace and joy which they breathe, prove attractive to every heart.
>
> The Prayer is short, that it may be quickly learned, easily remembered, and frequently used; but it contains all things pertaining to life and godliness. In its simplicity it seems adapted purposely for the weakness of the inexperienced and ignorant, and yet none can say that he is familiar with the heights and depths which it reveals, and with the treasures of wisdom it contains. It is calm, and suited to the even tenor of our daily life, and yet in times of trouble and conflict the Church has felt its value and power more especially, has discovered anew that it anticipates every difficulty and danger, that it solves every problem, and comforts the disciples of Christ in every tribulation of the world.
>
> It is the beloved and revered friend of our childhood, and it grows with our growth, a never-failing counselor and companion amid all the changing scenes of life. And as in our lifetime we must confess ourselves, with Luther, to be only learning the high and deep lessons of those petitions, so it will take eternity to give them their answer.[1]

The manifold perfections of the Lord's Prayer testify to the infinite wisdom of the Lord who taught us to pray. He gave us a wonderful prayer because he is a wonderful Savior.

This book is a practical exposition of the Lord's Prayer from Scripture. The more we pray, the more deeply we are drawn into communion with God. And the more we study the Lord's Prayer, the better we are able to pray. So perhaps an exposition such as this one can help us draw closer to our heavenly Father.

I am thankful that this book has been corrected and improved by the fine editorial staff at Crossway Books, and by many thoughtful suggestions from Cora Hogue, George McFarland, Maryann Modesti, and Jonathan Rockey. Nancy Ryken Taylor prepared the discussion questions, which were first tested in a small group Bible study at College Church in Wheaton, Illinois. But my greatest debt is to those friends and family members who pray for my preaching ministry. May God bless you for your faithfulness, and may this book help you when you pray!

1

How to Pray Like a Hypocrite

And when you pray, do not be like the hypocrites, for they love to pray standing in the synagogues and on the street corners to be seen by men. I tell you the truth, they have received their reward in full. But when you pray, go into your room, close the door and pray to your Father, who is unseen. Then your Father, who sees what is done in secret, will reward you.

MATTHEW 6:5-6

ONE OF THE GREAT CATHEDRALS of northern Europe displays an exquisite triptych of paintings on the life of prayer.[1] The first panel depicts the hustle and bustle of the daily marketplace. The scene is a large open square full of buying and selling, where merchants hawk their wares and greedy shoppers barter for bread. The second panel illustrates the prayers of the church. A handful of worshipers have stepped out of the marketplace and into the temple. White-robed priests are busy with their religious routines. They scurry to and fro, carrying oil for the lamps and water for the basin.

The third panel leaves behind the wranglings of the marketplace and the rituals of the temple and withdraws to the inner sanctuary. There, behind closed doors, a solitary worshiper kneels in the presence of God, privately and humbly to pray. The painting represents the hidden life of prayer and calls to mind the words of Jesus: "When you pray, go into your room, close the door and pray to your Father" (Matt. 6:6).

This series of paintings shows how rare it is to find a true man or woman of prayer. There are thousands out on the city streets and dozens at the church, but only one person inside the prayer closet. Of the thousands depicted, one individual enters the secret life of prayer.

TEACH US TO PRAY

Have you entered the secret life of prayer? Prayer is not just for spiritual giants; it is for ordinary Christians, too. Jesus' teaching about prayer in the Sermon on the Mount is intended for every one of his disciples. It is not so much a sermon as it is an invitation—an invitation to enter the secret life of prayer.

From the beginning, Jesus assumes two things about the prayer lives of his disciples. First, he assumes that we do pray. At least a little. Three times the phrase is repeated: "When you pray" (Matt. 6:5). "When you pray" (Matt. 6:6). "When you pray" (Matt. 6:7). Jesus knows that his disciples have at least begun to learn how to pray. And we do pray. We sense the necessity of prayer. We agree with Martin Luther that prayer is "the real calling of all Christians." We know that Andrew Murray is right when he calls prayer "the highest part of the work entrusted to us, the root and strength of all other work." So we pray, believing that no soul ever comes to a saving knowledge of Jesus Christ apart from prayer. We pray, knowing that there can be no effective preaching, no persuasive evangelism, no committed discipleship, no authentic mercy, and no cultural transformation without fervent prayer.

Yet we do not know how to pray as we ought. This is the second assumption Jesus makes about our prayer lives. He assumes that we need to be *taught* how to pray. Though it must grieve him, Jesus knows that prayerlessness is a common failing among his disciples. We pray . . . sometimes . . . but we still need to be instructed in prayer.

Many Christians who are serious about living for Christ struggle to pray. Not long ago a man asked me some hard questions about my prayer life. Often, we would rather not answer those kinds of questions. How is it between you and the Lord these days? What are you learning about God through prayer? What intimacy are you finding with God? When was the last time you really prayed?

How would you answer such questions? For many Christians, the secret life of prayer is a source of secret shame. The first disciples felt much the same way. They prayed, of course, but they did not know how to pray, at least very well. That explains why, in the Gospel of Luke, Jesus' teaching about prayer begins with an urgent request: "Lord, teach us to pray" (Luke 11:1). Not "teach us how to pray," notice, but "teach us to pray." Jesus went ahead and taught his disciples how to pray, but their request was more basic. Like us, the disciples more or less knew how to pray, but they still needed to learn to actually pray. Even the apostle Paul, who knew how to pray like he knew how to breathe, admitted that "we know not what we should pray for as we ought" (Rom. 8:26, KJV).

Jesus knows all this. That is why, when he invites us to enter the secret life of prayer, he begins with these words: "And when you pray, do not be like the hypocrites . . ." (Matt. 6:5). This was the verse that finally persuaded me to write this book on prayer. I have long been convinced, of course, of the absolute necessity of prayer for all spiritual life. Indeed, my goal as a minister is to keep the proclamation of God's Word and the prayers of God's people at the center of church life (see Acts 6:4). The great difficulty, however, is that this requires me to be a man of prayer as much as a preacher. I am learning to pray, but not so well that I feel I have very much to teach. Then I realized that I could begin where Jesus began, with a subject I know something about: the prayers of a hypocrite.

THE HYPOCRITE AT PRAYER

If Jesus tells us not to be like the hypocrites, we had better know who they are, and how they pray. The word *hypocrite* originally came from the theater. The Greek word *hypokrites* was the word for "actor," someone who played a part in a dramatic production. In the Greek theater, actors often wore masks to conceal their true identities. Thus, by Jesus' time, the word *hypocrite* was used for anyone who treated the world as his stage, casting himself in the starring role.

Jesus had seen some hypocrites at their prayers. If we had seen them, we undoubtedly would have been very impressed. On the outside, they gave every impression of being highly spiritual. According to Jesus, they *loved* to pray (Matt. 6:5). There can hardly be anything wrong with that! If only *we* loved to pray as much as they did!

These hypocrites loved to pray standing up. There is nothing wrong with that either. Hannah stood when she prayed for a son at the temple (1 Sam. 1:9-11). Jehoshaphat stood before the assembly to pray (2 Chron. 20:5). On at least one occasion, Jesus seemed to assume that his disciples would stand when they prayed (Mark 11:25). The Bible teaches that standing is one appropriate posture for prayer.

The hypocrites Jesus knew did not just stand anywhere, however; they prayed standing in the synagogues and on the street corners. So far, so good. There is nothing wrong with praying in a house of worship. Jesus went to the synagogue and called the temple a "house of prayer" (Luke 19:46). He also prayed when he was out in public. To give but one example, he prayed in front of the crowd that gathered at the tomb of Lazarus (John 11:41-42). Although Jesus condemned these hypocrites, there was nothing wrong with the frequency, the posture, or the location of their prayers.

The problem with these hypocrites was not *what* they did, but *why* they did it. "They love to pray standing in the synagogues and on the street corners *to be seen by men*" (Matt. 6:5). The last phrase is the most important one. As Augustine (354–430) explained, it is not "the being seen of men that is wrong, but doing these things for the purpose of being seen of men."[2] The problem with the hypocrite is his motivation. He does not want to be holy, he only wants to *seem* to be holy. He is more concerned with his reputation for righteousness than about actually becoming righteous. The approbation of men matters more to him than the approval of God. Hence, he positions his acts of piety for maximum effect; in this case, he prays at the corners of major intersections.

Since the hypocrite's prayer life is all for show, he is like the friar in a painting described by Spiros Zodhiates:

When the painting was viewed from a distance, one would think the friar was in a praying attitude. His hands were clasped together and held horizontally to his breast; his eyes meekly lowered, like those of the publican in the Gospel; and the good man appeared to be quite absorbed in humble adoration and devout recollection. But upon closer scrutiny, the deception vanished. The book that seemed to be before him was discovered to be a punch bowl into which the wretch was all the while only squeezing a lemon![3]

But God is not deceived. He is able to unmask the hypocrite. He can tell the difference between prayer offered to him and prayer offered for the benefit of humans.

Are you a hypocrite? One way to tell is to compare the amount of time you spend in private prayer to the amount of time you spend in public prayer. Some Christians pray for ten minutes on Sunday morning and ten minutes at Bible study and ten seconds before each meal, and that is about all. God does not measure our spirituality by a stopwatch. He does not clock our prayers. But surely there is something wrong if the only time we ever pray is when someone else is watching. As D. A. Carson rightly observes, "The person who prays more in public than in private reveals that he is less interested in God's approval than in human praise. Not piety but a reputation for piety is his concern."[4]

What is your concern—your piety, or your reputation for piety? My pastor in Scotland, the late Reverend William Still (1911–1997), used to say that when it comes to prayer, the church prayer meeting ought to be "the tip of the iceberg." That was good science as well as good Christianity. Only about 10 percent of an iceberg floats above the surface of the ocean, while the other 90 percent is submerged. In the same way, the public prayers of the church ought to be supported by a large mass of private prayer throughout the week. Unfortunately, the prayer life of the average Christian is more like the *Titanic* than an iceberg. We are proud vessels above the surface, but underneath our respectable Christianity, the bulkheads are filling with water, the pumps are failing, and we are in danger of sinking in a sea of spiritual neglect.

THE HYPOCRITE'S REWARD

Hypocrites pray to be seen. But what do they have to show for their prayers? Somewhat surprisingly, people who pray like hypocrites *are* rewarded for their efforts. Jesus says, "I tell you the truth, they have received their reward in full" (Matt. 6:5b).

God is perfectly just. He will give you as much as you deserve. If what you really want is the approval of other human beings, God will probably let you have it. You will gain the smug little satisfaction of thinking that you are more spiritual than others. But that is all you will get, which is why Jesus uses the perfect tense: "they *have received* their reward in full" (Matt. 6:5b). By the time the hypocrite says, "Amen," he has already received everything he will ever get for his prayers.

Jesus once told a story about the hypocrite's reward. It is the story of the Pharisee and the tax collector:

> *Two men went up to the temple to pray, one a Pharisee and the other a tax collector. The Pharisee stood up and prayed about himself: "God, I thank you that I am not like other men—robbers, evildoers, adulterers—or even like this tax collector. I fast twice a week and give a tenth of all I get."*
>
> *But the tax collector stood at a distance. He would not even look up to heaven, but beat his breast and said, "God, have mercy on me, a sinner."*
>
> LUKE 18:10-13

I wonder if the tax collector felt as if he had a very vibrant prayer life. I doubt he did. He certainly didn't feel close to God. He couldn't even bring himself to look up to heaven while he prayed, as was the custom. He could not approach God on the strength of his spiritual life—he could only come in the hope of God's mercy.

That is not how the Pharisee came. He felt he was doing rather well spiritually. He was giving. He was praying. He was fasting. As a result, he felt superior to all the other worshipers at the temple. But a feeling of superiority is all the old hypocrite ever received for his troubles. Jesus—who knew how to tell a good story—saved his punch line for the end. Concerning the tax collector, he said, "I tell you that this man, rather than the other, went home justified before God" (Luke 18:14a). However pleased he was with himself, the Pharisee did not have the pleasure of God. He went back home unjustified. He begged for attention rather than mercy, so at the end of the day he was still dead in his sins. He did not receive God's pardon for his transgressions.

Either you can have the approval of men or you can have the approbation of God, but not both. The problem with the hypocrite's reward is that it does not last very long. Human praise never does. Nor will it prove to be of much help on the day of judgment. When Christ returns as the glorious Judge, he will not read your letters of recommendation. He will not care how spiritual people *think* you are. He will know whether you have given him your heart or not. So unless the hypocrite's reward is all you want, do not be a hypocrite when you pray. Do not pretend to be what you are not; come as you are. Come the way the tax collector came, saying, "God, have mercy on me, a sinner" (Luke 18:13).

BEHIND CLOSED DOORS

The prayers of a true disciple are very different from the prayers of a hypocrite. To begin with, they are offered behind closed doors. Jesus says, "But when you pray, go into your room, close the door and pray to your Father" (Matt. 6:6). The word Jesus uses for room (*tameion*) is the word for a small inner closet or chamber. In those days, the storeroom was often the only room in the house with a door. The point is that every Christian should have a particular place to pray, preferably somewhere secret.

Not every Christian has a closet to pray in, but every Christian can find a private place to pray. In his wonderful little treatise on prayer, David M'Intyre describes a poor woman he met on the streets of one of Scotland's great cities. The demands of her work and the incessant clamor of the city made it difficult for her to find a quiet place to meet with her Lord. But eventually she found the perfect solution: "I throw my apron over my head," she said, "and *there* is my closet."[5] Another man M'Intyre mentions was converted on board a ship sailing back to Scotland from the West Indies. The ship was so crowded with sailors and passengers that there was no place to be alone. But the man still found a place to pray. "I can just cover my face with my hat," he said, "and I am as much alone with God as in a closet."[6]

Where do you pray? What place has become precious to you as the place where you meet with God? Is it a closet in your home? Do you go out into the woods to pray? Do you pray in the car on your way into the city? Or do you close the door to your office for ten minutes at lunch time? Wherever you pray, you unlock the treasure of intimate communion with God. The Puritan Samuel Lee (1627–1691?) wrote, "Prayer is the soul's colloquy with God, and secret prayer is a conference with God upon admission into the private chamber of heaven. When you have shut your own closet, when God and your soul are alone, with this key you open the chambers of paradise and enter the closet of divine love."[7]

Our great example for secret prayer, as for everything else, is the Lord Jesus Christ. He was always sneaking away from his disciples to pray in some secret place. We find this in all the Gospels. "Very early in the morning, while it was still dark, Jesus got up, left the house and went off to a solitary place, where he prayed" (Mark 1:35). "He went up on a mountainside by himself to pray. When evening came, he was there alone" (Matt. 14:23). "Jesus often withdrew to lonely places and prayed" (Luke 5:16). Even in the Garden of Gethsemane, when his disciples were with him, Jesus "withdrew about a stone's throw beyond them, knelt down, and prayed" (Luke 22:41). Throughout his ministry, right up to the time he prepared to die on the cross for our sins, Jesus went to pray in secret.

THE GOD WHO IS THERE

The reason Jesus went to the secret place is because his Father was there. That is precisely why he invites us to enter the secret life of prayer. He knows that God is in the secret place and will meet us there.

The *New International Version* translates Jesus' words like this:

"pray to your Father, who is unseen" (Matt. 6:6). It is true that God is unseen, for invisibility is one of his essential attributes. But in the original Greek this verse actually says something quite different. It says, "pray to your Father, who is in secret" (Matt. 6:6). God is not somewhere far away and inaccessible. No, he is right there in the secret place. Therefore, to step into the prayer closet is to commune with Almighty God. In order to emphasize the intimacy of secret prayer, Jesus describes the whole scene in personal terms: "your room . . . [your] door . . . your Father" (Matt. 6:6).

This promise of God's presence comes as a great encouragement. We are not always sure where our prayers are going. There are times in the Christian life when our prayers seem to bounce off the ceiling, when the door to heaven seems closed, even times when we wonder if we are just talking to ourselves. "Can you hear me, God? Are you still there?"

Our Savior—who went to the secret place so often himself—guarantees that God *is* there. "Your Father sees . . . what is done in secret" (Matt. 6:6). When we go to the secret place to pray, God will be waiting there to meet us. The unseen God is not unseeing. He not only sees, but he also hears. Therefore, when you pray, you are not simply talking to yourself, you are communicating with the God and Father of the Lord Jesus Christ. It was Cyprian (c. 200–258), the famous bishop of Carthage, who wrote, "In His teaching the Lord has bidden us to pray in secret—in hidden and remote places, in our very bedchambers—which is best suited to faith, that we may know that God is everywhere present, and hears and sees all, and in the plenitude of His majesty penetrates even into hidden and secret places."[8]

It is the promise of God's presence that helps most when we are weak in prayer. In his classic book *With Christ in the School of Prayer*, Andrew Murray writes,

> The Father is in secret: in these words Jesus teaches us where He is waiting us, where He is always to be found. Christians often complain that private prayer is not what it should be. They feel weak and sinful, the heart is cold and dark; it is as if they have so little to pray, and in that little no faith or joy.

They are discouraged and kept from prayer by the thought
that they cannot come to the Father as they ought or as they
wish. Child of God! listen to your Teacher. He tells you that
when you go to private prayer your first thought must be: The
Father is in secret, the Father waits me there. Just because
your heart is cold and prayerless, get you into the presence of
the loving Father.[9]

REWARD!

Those who go to meet with God in the secret place will be rewarded
for their efforts. Jesus mentions this three times in his Sermon on the
Mount. His instructions about giving, praying, and fasting all end
with the same promise: "your Father, who sees what is done in
secret, will reward you" (Matt. 6:4, 6, 18). The Christian life is very
rewarding.

What kind of reward does Jesus have in mind? Since God is our
heavenly Father, it might be a heavenly reward, to be received at the
last day. In fact, Jesus gives the distinct impression that God grants
rewards over and above the free gift of eternal life. He does not spec-
ify what kind of reward will be given to those who pray in secret, but
it is enough to know that the reward comes from the hand of a gracious God.

Another reward for meeting with God in the secret place is
answered prayer. This is perhaps the greatest difference between the
prayer of a hypocrite and the prayer of a true believer. "Prayers which
are meant for the ears of others will never reach the ears of God."[10]
Only a prayer that is truly offered to God will be heard and answered.
People who meet with God in the secret place can expect to get some
answers. This was the experience of the tax collector at the temple.
There was only one thing he asked God to do, and that was to have
mercy on his soul. His prayers were answered. The man went home
justified because God forgave all his sins. God's reward for those who
meet with him in secret is answered prayer. It is said that the missionary called "Praying Hyde" (1865–1912) recorded some 50,000
specific answers to his prayers. What is your experience with

answered prayer? If you have asked God to have mercy on your soul, you are off to a good start. Your prayer has been answered. Anyone who comes to God, asking for mercy and trusting in Jesus Christ, receives the free gift of eternal life.

Finally, true prayer is its own reward. The reward for secret prayer is the prayer itself, the blessing of resting in the presence of God. Prayer does not simply maintain the Christian life, *it is* the Christian life, reduced to its barest essence. Can there be any greater joy—in this life or the next—than to commune in the secret place with the living God?

One man who had a rewarding prayer life was the father of Dr. John Paton (1824–1907), the great Scottish missionary to the New Hebrides. Paton's father was a simple man, a stocking-maker by trade. Although the family lived in a small cottage, he kept a private place to pray. Paton described it like this:

> The closet was a very small apartment . . . having room only for a bed, a little table, and a chair, with a diminutive window shedding a diminutive light on the scene. This was the sanctuary of that cottage home. There daily, and many times a day, generally after each meal, we saw our father retire, and—shut to the door; and we children got to understand, by a sort of spiritual instinct (for the thing was too sacred to be talked about), that prayers were being poured out there for us, as of old by the High Priest within the veil in the Most Holy Place. We occasionally heard the pathetic echoes of a trembling voice, pleading as for life, and we learned to slip out and in past that door on tip-toe, not to disturb the holy charge. The outside world might not know, but we knew, whence came that happy light, as of a new-born smile, that always was dawning on my father's face: it was a reflection from the Divine Presence, in the consciousness of which he lived.[11]

Paton's father went to the secret place, where his own Father was always waiting. There he earned his reward: not only the assurance of eternal life and the hope of answered prayer, but also the surpassing joy of communing with the triune God.

For Discussion

1. What analogies or images help you understand true prayer? For example, perhaps it helps you to imagine yourself climbing onto the Father's lap as a child would do.

2. When or where is it easiest for you to pray? When or where is it hardest?

3. Read Matthew 6:5-6. What is a hypocrite?

4. According to these verses, what are the characteristics of hypocrites' prayers?

5. What is the key difference between hypocrites' and believers' prayers?

6. What is the key difference between hypocrites' and believers' rewards?

7. The Greek translation of verse 6 reads, "pray to your Father, who is in secret." How does the secret-ness of God relate to Jesus' command not to pray like a hypocrite?

8. Jesus says that the prayers of true disciples are offered behind closed doors (Matt. 6:6). What are the spiritual advantages of secret prayer? What godly character traits does secret prayer foster that cannot be learned through public prayer?

9. D. A. Carson observes that "The person who prays more in public than in private reveals that he is less interested in God's approval than in human praise. Not piety but a reputation for piety is his concern" ("Matthew," *Expositor's Bible Commentary*, 8:165). Do you agree or disagree with this criterion? Explain your answer.

10. Do your prayer habits suggest that your motive in prayer is the approval of other people or a desire to be intimate with God? What can you do to increase your desire for and experience of intimacy with God?

11. Jesus told a parable to hypocrites who trusted in their own righteousness and looked down on others. Read Luke 18:9-14. How would you describe each of the men in this parable?

12. The Pharisee in this story had a lot to be proud of. Why wasn't he justified before God?

13. Based on the words and actions of the tax collector, what characterizes true humility?

14. In verse 14 Jesus summarizes the message of this parable. From other parts of Scripture or your own experiences, give examples of God humbling the proud and honoring the humble. What methods does he use?

15. If you were listening to Jesus tell this parable, what might you think and feel?

16. Most of us sometimes pray more like the Pharisee and other times are truly humble like the tax collector. What would be some signals that you were praying more like the Pharisee than the tax collector?

2

$\mathcal{H}ow\ to\ \mathcal{P}ray\ \mathcal{L}ike\ an\ Orphan$

And when you pray, do not keep on babbling like pagans,
for they think they will be heard because of their many words.
Do not be like them, for your Father knows
what you need before you ask him.
MATTHEW 6:7-8

AS I TRAVELED TO ANOTHER COUNTRY, I fell asleep and then awoke to a strange sound. A group of men had gathered in the back of the airplane to say their prayers to a strange god in a foreign language. Their prayers were incessant. Louder and louder they babbled, constantly repeating the same phrases over and over again. It was almost frightening, especially after a deep sleep.

I suppose the men were offering the kind of prayer Jesus described in his Sermon on the Mount. Having warned his disciples about the dangers of *ostentatious* prayer (Matt. 6:5-6), he proceeded to warn them about the dangers of *repetitious* prayer:[1] "And when you pray, do not keep on babbling like pagans" (Matt. 6:7).

PAGANS AT PRAYER

The Bible does not indicate when Jesus was exposed to other religions, but at some time or other he had heard pagans say their prayers. What he had noticed especially was how repetitious they were. The King

James Version puts it like this: "But when ye pray, use not vain repetitions, as the heathen do" (Matt. 6:7a KJV).

When Jesus criticized the prayers of the heathen, he was not objecting to them praying in different languages. God has been hearing multi-lingual prayers since the Tower of Babel. The reason Jesus came into the world was to "purchase men for God from every tribe and language and people and nation" (Rev. 5:9). It is God's desire to be praised in every language on the face of the earth. Nor is there anything wrong with long prayers. Jesus objected to people who kept on praying and praying in order to show off (Mark 12:40), of course, but there are some fairly lengthy prayers in the Bible—Psalm 119, for example, or Ezra's prayer when he sat down to mourn for a whole day (Ezra 9:1–10:1). Jesus himself sometimes prayed all through the night (Luke 6:12).

The problem with the pagans was not that they prayed in a foreign language or that they prayed too long, but that they prayed the same thing over and over and over again. The prayers of the ancient Greeks and Romans were verbose. Some recited incantations to appease the gods. Others repeated magical phrases in an attempt to manipulate events in their favor. Pagan prayers were good luck charms full of empty phrases.

The Greeks and the Romans were not the only ones who babbled their prayers. People continue to utter meaningless prayers to this very day. For example, the Hindus babble their prayers when they repeat their *mantras*. A *mantra* is simply the name of a Hindu god, or some other phrase, uttered over and over again, until the mind becomes comfortably numb. Babbling is also a potential danger in using a rosary or having a fixed liturgy for prayer. The same phrases are mumbled so frequently that they cease to have any meaning. But the prayer babbled more than any other is probably the Lord's Prayer. How ironic! Jesus gave us the Lord's Prayer so we could learn to pray sincerely, not mindlessly. Yet Christians often use it without even thinking about what it means. They *say* the Lord's Prayer without actually *praying* it.

Begging for an Answer

The reason pagans babble the way they do is because they are not sure whether God will hear them. "They think they will be heard because of their many words" (Matt. 6:7b). When the Greeks and Romans prayed, they often began by reciting long lists of the names of their deities, hoping that one of them would answer. Since their gods were not all-seeing, all-knowing, or all-loving, people were never sure if they would get an answer or not. So the longer they prayed, the better. If they prayed long enough or hard enough or used just the right words, perhaps one of their gods would answer.

To describe the situation another way, pagans babble their prayers because they are orphans. The tragedy of a child without a father is that he or she can never depend on a father's love. An orphan never learns what it is like to be tucked into bed by a loving father, or to hear the promise of unconditional love: "You are my precious child, you have been my precious child, and you will always be my precious child."

As a result of being raised without a father's love, many orphans have nagging doubts about their identity. Secretly, they invent stories about their fathers coming to rescue them. They are so starved for affection that they cling to it wherever they can find it. Yet they are never secure in that love. They always need to test it, and sometimes they even run from it.

Some friends of mine have opened their home to the needy street children of Brazil, many of whom are orphans. One day my friends went into Sao Paulo on business. As they walked through the city they noticed a boy huddled with a blanket. There was something vaguely familiar about him, and as they drew closer they realized that they knew the boy. He had lived in their home for a while; then—suddenly—he had disappeared. They were so overjoyed to see the boy again that they ran to be reunited with him. After they had embraced, they asked him, "Why did you run away?" The boy answered sadly, "I didn't think you wanted me to stay."

The truth, of course, was exactly the opposite. The boy had been deeply loved and dearly cared for. Yet because he was an orphan, he never felt secure in that love. He was not absolutely certain in his heart of hearts that he was wanted. So the boy left home to become a beggar on the streets.

Begging is exactly what many postmodern pagans do when they pray. They pray like orphans. They may not pray very often, but when they do, it usually takes the form of begging. In their heart of hearts they do not know for certain that God loves them. As a result, they think they have to beg for everything they can get. They pray when they are desperate—teetering on the verge of bankruptcy, perhaps, or facing major surgery. When all else fails, they will pray, "Please, God. I don't know if you're there or not, but if you are, help me out just this once. I'm begging you. If you get me out of this one I'll try to be a better person from now on." Like most forms of begging, such prayers are piteously desperate.

The reason some people pray like spiritual orphans is because they have not yet given their hearts to Jesus Christ. Jesus said, "I am the way and the truth and the life. No one comes to the Father except through me. If you really knew me, you would know my Father as well" (John 14:6-7a). What could be plainer than that? The only way to experience the love of God the Father is to respond to the love of God the Son. Anyone who believes that Jesus Christ is the Son of God and the Savior of the world gets everything he has to offer—the forgiveness of sins, the promise of eternal life, and all the rest of it, including the right to become a child of God. Theologians call this the doctrine of adoption. Anyone who comes to Jesus Christ in faith becomes a child of God by legal adoption. The *Westminster Shorter Catechism* defines it well: "Adoption is an act of God's free grace, whereby we are received into the number, and have a right to all the privileges, of the sons of God" (A. 34).

This privilege of becoming God's own son or daughter is not granted to everyone; it is only for those who put their trust in Jesus Christ. "To all who received him, to those who believed in his name, he gave the right to become children of God" (John 1:12). "You are all sons of God through faith in Christ Jesus" (Gal. 3:26). If your prayers sound more like the beggings of an orphan than the askings of a son, this may be the reason: Adoption takes place for those who believe in Jesus Christ. Perhaps the time has finally come for you to become a true child of God through faith in Jesus Christ.

WHEN A CHILD ACTS LIKE AN ORPHAN

Pagans are not the only ones who pray like orphans. Sometimes Christians pray like orphans, too, even though they have been adopted into God's family. Some Christians may secretly doubt that God loves them. They don't want to ask for too much because they are afraid that God might not answer their prayers. When it comes right down to it, they are not absolutely certain of God's fatherly care. They feel as if they have to talk God into giving them what they need. They think they have to pray in exactly the right way or for precisely the right amount of time to get God to hear them.

Why do God's children still pray like orphans? Many times, it is because of sin. Whenever a child rebels against his father there is a rupture in their relationship. In the same way, Christians who sin against their heavenly Father are bound to feel like orphans. In other cases, Christians pray like orphans because they have never experienced an earthly father's love. Some may have been raised by fathers who never established a vital, loving presence in the home. Others may never have had a father at home at all. America has now embarked on a foolhardy experiment to discover what happens to a culture in which nearly half the children do not live with their fathers. One result is that many people do not know how to call God "Father," nor do they want to.

Human fathers have always had their limitations. Perhaps that is why Jesus spent so much time teaching his disciples what it means to have a heavenly Father. He speaks about his Father dozens and dozens of times in the Gospels (e.g., Matt. 11:25-26; John 10:30; 14:10ff.) because he knew that it is impossible to know God until you come to know him as Father. In his teaching on prayer, especially, Jesus introduces his disciples to their heavenly Father. "Your heavenly Father is perfect" (Matt. 5:48). "Your Father . . . will reward you" (Matt. 6:4, 6, 18). "Your Father knows what you need" (Matt. 6:8). "Your heavenly

Father will also forgive you" (Matt. 6:14). Jesus teaches that when we enter the family of God, our adoptive Father is perfect, generous, thoughtful, and forgiving.

KEEP IT SIMPLE

Having the perfect Father makes all the difference when it comes time to pray. Knowing God as Father has two tremendous implications for the life of prayer. First, it means that you can keep it simple; second, it means that God will give you what you need almost before you ask.

First, you can keep prayer simple. When children need something from their fathers, they do not hire a lawyer, draft a formal petition, or get down on their knees, they just ask. That is why Christian prayers are straightforward. The prayers of pagans tend to be overly complicated, but when Christians pray, they pray to their Father.

As a general rule, the prayers of God's children are short and sweet. Martin Luther (1483–1546) once said, "Our prayer must have few words, but be great and profound in content and meaning. . . . Few words and richness of meaning is Christian; many words and lack of meaning is pagan."[2] Indeed, one of the striking things about most biblical prayers is their brevity. It is hard to find a prayer anywhere in the Bible that when read aloud would be more than five minutes long. Some Christians measure spirituality by the amount of time a person prays. True, there is plenty of teaching in Scripture about being devoted to the life of prayer. Jesus himself spent a great deal of time in prayer, and the apostle Paul tells us to "pray without ceasing" (1 Thess. 5:17, KJV). However, the effectiveness of our prayers does not depend on the length of our prayers.

One of the best examples of the power of a simple prayer is the story of Elijah on Mount Carmel. The great prophet gathered the people of Israel on the mountain for a prayer meeting. All the prophets of Baal were on one side, Elijah on the other . . . and may the best prayer win.

According to the rules of the contest, each side was to place a bull on their altar and ask their deity to receive their sacrifice. Elijah said,

"You call on the name of your god, and I will call on the name of the LORD. The god who answers by fire—he is God" (1 Kings 18:24a). Elijah was giving the prophets of Baal the "home bull advantage," so they went first. They chose their bull, placed it on their altar, and started to pray to their god. "They called on the name of Baal from morning till noon. 'O Baal, answer us!' they shouted. But there was no response; no one answered" (1 Kings 18:26b). So they kept on praying. The longer those pagans prayed, the wilder they became. "They shouted louder and slashed themselves with swords and spears, as was their custom, until their blood flowed. Midday passed, and they continued their frantic prophesying until the time for the evening sacrifice. But there was no response, no one answered, no one paid attention" (1 Kings. 18:28-29). After six hours of prayer, they still had nothing to show for it.

Then Elijah stood up. As the people gathered around him he repaired the Lord's altar. Once the sacrifice had been arranged, the prophet stepped forward and offered the simplest of prayers: "O LORD, God of Abraham, Isaac and Israel, let it be known today that you are God in Israel and that I am your servant and have done all these things at your command. Answer me, O LORD, answer me, so these people will know that you, O LORD, are God, and that you are turning their hearts back again" (1 Kings 18:36b-37).

That was all Elijah prayed. He did not babble on all day. He did not make vain repetitions or use empty phrases. He didn't need to— he was speaking to his Father. All he needed to do was make a simple request. Once his prayer was finished, he received a straightforward answer. "Then the fire of the LORD fell and burned up the sacrifice, the wood, the stones and the soil, and also licked up the water in the trench" (1 Kings 18:38). The mighty conflagration proved the difference between the endless prayers of the pagans and the simple request of a child of God.

God does not need any lengthy explanations. If you find that your prayer life is weak, is it possible that you are trying to make things too complicated? Our prayers must be fervent, of course, and they ought to be frequent, but they do not need to be fancy.

ALMOST BEFORE YOU ASK

The reason the prayers of God's children can be simple is that our Father is so well-informed. He is all-knowing; therefore, he already knows what we need. He knows about it even before we need it. And because he is our loving Father, he often supplies what we need almost before we ask.

God does not learn any new information from our prayers. He does not sit on his throne, saying, "Eh, what's that? What did you say you need? Really? I hadn't the foggiest idea!" God never says that because he always knows what we need. In the whole history of the world, God has never once been surprised during a prayer meeting. So there is no need to beg (although there is a place for persistence, as Jesus taught on another occasion; Luke 18:1-8). Begging is for pagans, who can only hope they will be heard for their many words. "Do not be like them," Jesus says, "for your Father knows what you need before you ask him" (Matt. 6:8).

There is a story in the Old Testament about a father who knew what his son needed even before he asked. As it happens, it is also a story about adoption. It is the story of Mephibosheth, the son of Jonathan and the grandson of King Saul.

Mephibosheth had survived a tragic childhood. Both his father and grandfather were slain in battle. When the news arrived of their brutal demise, the whole palace was thrown into a panic. In the confusion, Mephibosheth's "nurse picked him up and fled, but as she hurried to leave, he fell and became crippled" (2 Sam. 4:4b). As a result of this tragic series of events, the boy became an orphan and he was lame in both legs.

Yet eventually Mephibosheth was shown a father's love. Some time later, after David had become king, he asked, "Is there anyone still left of the house of Saul to whom I can show kindness for Jonathan's sake?" (2 Sam. 9:1). David was informed that one of Jonathan's sons was still alive, although a cripple. So the king had Mephibosheth brought to the palace.

> *When Mephibosheth son of Jonathan, the son of Saul, came to David, he bowed down to pay him honor.*
>
> *David said, "Mephibosheth!"*
>
> *"Your servant," he replied.*
>
> *"Don't be afraid," David said to him, "for I will surely show you kindness for the sake of your father Jonathan. I will restore to you all the land that belonged to your grandfather Saul, and you will always eat at my table."*
>
> 2 SAMUEL 9:6-7

When David offered all this lovingkindness, it was hard for Mephibosheth to accept. He was an orphan, after all, so it was hard for him to feel secure in the king's love. Mephibosheth bowed down and said, "What is your servant, that you should notice a dead dog like me?" (2 Sam. 9:8). But David loved Mephibosheth like his own son, so he did everything he promised. He gave him back his land. Recognizing that Mephibosheth had a disability, he not only gave him land, he also arranged for servants to farm it. He even welcomed him at the palace like a prince; "so Mephibosheth ate at David's table like one of the king's sons" (2 Sam. 9:11b).

The amazing thing is that David took care of everything Mephibosheth needed even before he had a chance to ask. That is what a father does, especially an adoptive father. A father knows what his children need, even before they ask, and he helps them as soon as he can.

As a father, I find that my children often make requests I have already granted: "Hey, Dad, can we take our baseball stuff to the park?" "Of course we can," I say, "but you know what, I already put it in the car!" "Can I have some milk, Daddy?" my daughter asks. And she will have her milk as soon as she asks, because—unbeknownst to her—I have already taken a cup from the shelf, poured the milk, and put the carton back into the refrigerator.

If it is true that human parents know what their children need before they ask, at least sometimes, it is all the more true of our heavenly Father: "If you, then, though you are evil, know how to give good gifts to your children, how much more will your Father in heaven give good gifts to those who ask him!" (Matt. 7:11). What do you need? Comfort? Healing? Guidance? Housing? Employment? Whatever the need, if you are a child of God, your Father is probably working to meet it at this very moment. Very likely, he has begun a providential series of events that ultimately will result in the answer to your prayers.

Hudson Taylor (1832–1905), the great missionary to China, learned that God gives us what we need almost before we ask. In 1859 Taylor faced a crisis. The man who ran his mission hospital suddenly was forced to return to England. Unfortunately, the man not only ran the hospital, but he also provided almost all its funding. The future of the work was in jeopardy.

Hudson Taylor did not have any idea how God would provide for the hospital, but he was absolutely convinced that God would provide. To close the mission down would be to fail God's calling. Taylor called the hospital staff together to explain the situation. Among other things, he told them that he could no longer guarantee their salaries. Yet he invited them to stay and to trust God for their needs. Some doubted and returned home, but others were willing to depend on God's fatherly care.

Gradually, the situation at the hospital worsened. The food supply decreased, until finally they were down to their last bag of rice. Then, on the day their food ran out altogether, a letter arrived from England with a check for fifty pounds, and the hospital was saved. Furthermore, the man who wrote the check had recently come into a large inheritance, and wanted to know how the rest of the money could be used to glorify God in the land of China. The remarkable thing is not simply that God kept the hospital open. The remarkable thing is that the letter had been sent months before it arrived in China, long before the crisis began. God knew about the need before the need arose, so by the time Hudson Taylor prayed for God's help, help was already on its way.[3]

Our heavenly Father loves to take care of his children. If there is something you need—really need—all you need to do is ask. You do not need to beg, borrow, or steal. You do not need to say a magic prayer. Just tell your Father what you need. He already knows all about it, and very likely, help is already on the way.

For Discussion

1. Why do you think Jesus told his disciples not to "babble" like the pagans? What is the danger in such prayers?

2. What types of repetition are appropriate in a true disciple's prayer?

3. Read Matthew 6:7-8. What are some reasons people use repetitive prayers?

4. What do "babbled" prayers like the ones Jesus warns against indicate about the one who prays them?

5. Jesus says that the primary reason not to use repetitious or wordy prayers is because God knows what we need before we ask him. Why, and in what ways, does believing that God already knows what you need before you ask change the way you pray?

6. If God already knows our needs, why should we pray?

7. How can people who use set prayers or liturgies in their prayer life safeguard against the dangers of repetitious prayer?

8. Are you ever tempted to pray repetitious prayers? How can you remind yourself in those situations that God knows what you need even before you ask?

9. Jesus told a parable about God's fatherly care for orphans in Luke 15:11-32. As you read it, put yourself in the shoes of the son who chose to be an orphan and the father who knew what he needed before he asked. What words would you use to describe the younger son?

10. Why did the son return to his father? Do you think he expected to be forgiven? Why or why not?

11. What does the father in this story show us about God?

12. In what ways is God unlike the father in this story?

13. What do you know about the older brother from this story?

14. How might knowing that God is much like the father in this story affect the way you pray?

15. If you think of the father in this story as a model of love, the younger son as a prodigal returning home, and the older son as a pious but resentful Christian, which of the three characters in this story best represents your spiritual state right now, and why?

16. What symptoms indicate that someone is acting like a spiritual orphan?

17. What symptoms indicate spiritual snobbery like that of the older son in this story?

18. What are some practical ways to prevent yourself from praying the babbling prayers of a spiritual orphan?

3

How to Pray Like God's Own Dear Child

This, then, is how you should pray . . .
MATTHEW 6:9a

JESUS' TEACHING ON PRAYER in the Sermon on the Mount follows a logical order. He begins with a warning against *ostentatious* prayer (Matt. 6:5-6). Instead of praying in order to be seen—the way hypocrites do—Jesus teaches us to pray in secret. Second, he warns against *repetitious* prayer (Matt. 6:7-8). Instead of babbling on and on like a pagan or begging like an orphan, Jesus teaches us to tell our Father what we need.

All of this prepares the way for what Jesus teaches about *efficacious* prayer. That prayer which is uniquely effective for releasing God's blessing in the world is, of course, the Lord's Prayer. Here is the prayer Jesus taught his disciples, in its most familiar form:

> *Our Father which art in heaven, Hallowed be thy name. Thy kingdom come. Thy will be done in earth, as it is in heaven. Give us this day our daily bread. And forgive us our debts, as we forgive our debtors. And lead us not into temptation, but deliver us from evil: For thine is the kingdom, and the power, and the glory, for ever. Amen.*
> MATTHEW 6:9-13, KJV

It is little wonder that these simple words of Jesus have become the world's most famous prayer. The Lord's Prayer is, as Dietrich

Bonhoeffer (1906–1945) once said, "the quintessence of prayer."[1] Yet for all their simplicity, the petitions that make up the Lord's Prayer are profound in their theology. As Cyprian marveled so long ago, "What matters of deep moment are contained in the Lord's prayer! How many and how great, briefly collected in the words, but spiritually abundant in virtue! so that there is absolutely nothing passed over that is not comprehended in these our prayers and petitions, as in a compendium of heavenly doctrine."[2] Much more recently, Ernst Lohmeyer has observed in his comprehensive study of the prayer that "in fixed and perfectly-chosen words the Lord's Prayer offers an inexhaustible content, which can always be grasped and repeated by the prayers of heart and mouth, yet never fathomed in the thoughts of the mind."[3]

THE FAMILY PRAYER

Before studying each individual phrase in the Lord's Prayer, we need to look at the prayer as a whole. What do we notice when we do?

Although the Lord's Prayer is simple, its structure has been analyzed in various ways. The phrase "Our Father in heaven" is usually considered the preface, and the part about God's kingdom, power, and glory is obviously the conclusion, but there are different ways of organizing the middle. Augustine and Martin Luther, among others, divided verse 13 in half ("And lead us not into temptation"; "But deliver us from the Evil One"). As a result, they ended up with a preface and seven petitions, followed by a conclusion. Many other commentators have followed John Calvin in keeping verse 13 together so as to have six petitions.[4]

However the Lord's Prayer is divided, almost everyone recognizes that it moves from God's glory to our good. As Kent Hughes writes, "The initial focus of this model prayer is upward, as its first three requests have to do with God's glory. Then, having prayed for His glory, the remaining three requests are for our well-being. God first, humans second. That is the ideal order of prayer: His glory before our wants."[5] We do not pray about our debts or our daily bread until we have prayed for God's name, God's kingdom, and God's will. Nor do our wants get the last word. The Lord's Prayer properly closes with God's kingdom, God's power, and God's glory. Thus, like everything else in the whole universe, the prayer ends where it began: with the glory of God.

I have never heard anyone pray the Lord's Prayer with a larger sense of God's glory than my grandfather. Few memories are more precious to me than hearing him pray at the family dinner table. Often he would use the words of the Lord's Prayer. From the very first phrase—when he said, "Our Father"—to the very last word— "Amen!"—he ushered our family into the presence of God in all his glory. My grandfather prayed so fervently that it seemed as if he were praying these words for the very first time.

When I was very young I thought my grandfather's words were the exclusive property of our family. I learned them from my father, who learned them from his father, and so on. This was the way the Rykens prayed. Eventually, of course, I discovered that other Christians pray this way, too. The Lord's Prayer is a family prayer for all God's children, whether they learned to pray it at home or not.

TALK TO YOUR FATHER

There are three important ways in which the Lord's Prayer is a family prayer. The first is the most obvious: in it we pray to our Father.

It must have been tremendously important to Jesus that his disciples learn to call God "Father." In his brief instructions on prayer, Jesus mentions the Father six times. Hypocrites pray so that others can hear them. Pagans are not sure whether anyone will hear them or not. But Christians pray to their Father. We pray to the Father who meets with us in the secret place (Matt. 6:6). We pray to the Father who knows what we need even before we ask him (Matt. 6:8). We pray to the Father who is in heaven, ruling over all the earth (Matt. 6:9). And we pray to the Father who forgives our sins, for Jesus' sake (Matt. 6:14). The fatherhood of God keeps coming up in these verses because Jesus keeps bringing it up. No one can learn to pray who does not learn to call God "Father." That is what prayer is; it is talking with your Father.

Over the years, the fatherhood of God has come to shape my own prayer life. When I pray, I nearly always address God as "Father." I do not do this by any particular design; it is simply how I pray. Undoubtedly, this is the way I pray because this is the way Jesus has taught me to pray. It is the way Jesus has taught you to pray as well. Realize that your fundamental identity as a Christian is that you are a son or a daughter of the Most High God. Therefore, when you pray—whether you use our family prayer or not—address God as your Father.

PRAYING IN THE PLURAL

There is a second sense in which the Lord's Prayer is a family prayer. The Father to whom we pray is called *our* Father. This means that when we pray, we are joined by our brothers and sisters. As the *Westminster Shorter Catechism* puts it, "we should pray with and for others" (A. 100).

Because this is something we learn from the precise wording of the Lord's Prayer, it is important to realize that there is more to the Lord's Prayer than mere words. Jesus was teaching his disciples *how* to pray, not *what* to pray. He did not say, "Pray *this*:" and then give the exact words we always have to use in our prayers. Instead, he said, "Pray like this," or "Pray in this manner."

It is worth remembering that the Lord's Prayer is not the only prayer God has given the church. All the prayers in Scripture are inspired by the Holy Spirit. The words of Moses, or David, or Mary are also suitable for public and private worship. Yet the Lord's Prayer does establish a pattern for prayer. It has a special role in establishing our model for acceptable prayer. As the *Shorter Catechism* explains, "The whole word of God is of use to direct us in prayer; but the special rule of direction is that form of prayer which Christ taught his disciples, commonly called *The Lord's prayer*" (A. 99).

The fact that Jesus gave his disciples a flexible pattern helps to explain why the version of the prayer found in Luke 11:2-4 is different from the version found in Matthew 6. There are different words, different phrases, even different petitions altogether.

The reason for these differences has been hotly debated since the early church.[6] Some have wondered whether Matthew was adding to

Luke, or Luke was subtracting from Matthew, or even if there is a contradiction between the two of them. The obvious answer is that Jesus taught his disciples to pray on at least two different occasions. In Matthew, the Lord's Prayer is part of the Sermon on the Mount. In Luke, it is given as an answer to a question from one of the disciples ("Lord, teach us to pray, just as John taught his disciples"—Luke 11:1b). That there should be two versions shouldn't be surprising. Like most good teachers, when Jesus had something important to say, he said it more than once. But he did not always repeat himself word for word. The fact that he taught two slightly different versions of the Lord's Prayer shows that he did not expect his disciples to repeat him word for word, either.

The Lord's Prayer is a flexible pattern or framework for prayer, what Tertullian (c. 165–c. 215) called "a new outline of prayer."[7] Not that it is wrong to repeat the prayer word for word, of course. It is good to use the very words of Christ, and the Lord's Prayer should be a regular part of both public and private worship. But the Lord gives us the freedom to improvise our own words when we pray, provided that we stay within his guidelines for prayer.

The petitions in the Lord's Prayer are something like the courses for dinner at a fine restaurant. The waiter will offer an appetizer, a soup, a salad, a meat, and a dessert. Each diner has choices to make— vegetable soup or minestrone? house dressing or vinaigrette? beef or fish?—but the same courses are always served, and in the same order. In a similar way, the petitions in the Lord's Prayer establish the menu for prayer. Adoration, submission, supplication, confession, intercession, and exaltation—these are the courses that make up a prayer. Every true prayer is drawn from the same basic outline. Hugh Latimer (1485–1555), the English reformer who was martyred for his faith, said, "this prayer [is] the sum and abridgment of all other prayers. All other prayers are contained in this prayer; yea, whatsoever mankind hath need of as to soul and body, that same is contained in this prayer."[8]

Even though Jesus gave his disciples a prayer to imitate rather than a prayer to memorize, he did give us specific words to use when we pray. Since Jesus undoubtedly chose his words with care, it is important to notice what he repeats over and over again: the first person plural pronouns "our" and "us." "*Our* Father." "Give *us*." "Forgive *us*." "Deliver *us*." The Lord's Prayer is for the whole family of God.

Someone has written a clever poem to help remind us that the Lord's Prayer is not for rugged individualists:

> *You cannot pray the Lord's Prayer*
> *And even once say "I."*
> *You cannot say the Lord's Prayer*
> *And even once say "My."*
> *Nor can you pray the Lord's Prayer*
> *And not pray for another,*
> *For when you ask for daily bread*
> *You must include your brother.*
> *For others are included*
> *in each and every plea—*
> *From the beginning to the end of it,*
> *It never once says "Me!"*[9]

There is a time—and a place—for private prayer. The time is frequently, and the place is in your closet. Jesus mentioned this when he was speaking about the dangers of ostentatious prayer: "But when you pray, go into your room, close the door and pray to your Father, who is unseen" (Matt. 6:6). All the great men and women of the Bible—such as Moses, Hannah, and Daniel—excelled in the secret life of prayer. Jesus himself often went to pray—alone—in the solitary wilderness (e.g., Mark 1:35; Luke 5:16).

Yet God does not expect us to maintain the life of prayer in our own strength. Jesus knows how weak we are. Therefore, when he teaches us to pray, he invites us into fellowship. He has given us a family prayer, a prayer we must be taught by another Christian. Furthermore, the prayer itself assumes that we will have company when we pray. When we offer prayer to our Father, we will be joined by our spiritual brothers and sisters. As Luther said, "The Lord's prayer binds the people together, and knits them one to another, so that one prays *for* another, and together *with* one another."[10]

To pray is to practice the communion of the saints, which is the spiritual fellowship all Christians everywhere enjoy in Jesus Christ. Spiros Zodhiates writes:

> . . . in prayer *I am not alone*. I am one with the members of God's family, which is also my family. My weak prayer is caught up into the great stream of prayer that goes up forever from God's family. The strength of my prayer is that it is not simply mine; that the moment I fall upon my knees I am no longer an individual man or woman talking to God, but a member of the family of God, a sharer in that human nature which Christ has carried to the right hand of God.
>
> The communion of saints is what gives life and force to prayer, comfort and confidence to those who pray. *On my knees I cannot be alone.* My prayer, as weak, as feeble, as helpless as it is, is organically united with the prayers of the whole Church. We are all members of one body. We belong to an association for intercessory prayer.[11]

PRAY WITH YOUR BROTHERS AND SISTERS

Jesus often took a small group of disciples with him when he went off to pray. Before he was transfigured, "he took Peter, John and James with him and went up onto a mountain to pray" (Luke 9:28). He took his disciples to watch and pray with him in the Garden of Gethsemane (Matt. 26:36-38). To this very day, Jesus calls all his disciples to come away in small groups to pray, for wherever two or three come together in his name, he is right there with them (Matt. 18:20).

Since Jesus has commanded us to pray together, we should pray in our homes. Christian roommates should pray together—daily if possible, but at least weekly. Parents should pray with their children at mealtimes, at bedtime, and throughout the day. Husbands and wives should pray together about the needs of their household.

Christians should also pray together in small groups. Home Bible studies and fellowship groups are sometimes considered a recent development in the life of the church. Yet wise Christians have never been satisfied to worship only once a week. They have always gathered during the week for prayer. The first apostles went to the temple to pray. The apostle Paul held house meetings in all the churches he planted. Even under persecution, Christians met in places like the catacombs to pray. Societies of men and women were organized for prayer throughout the Middle Ages. During the Reformation, pastors met together for Bible teaching and prayer. Many of the Puritans formed house groups. In short, Christians have always met regularly to pray with their brothers and sisters. If prayer meetings were good enough for people like Peter, Lydia, Bernard of Clairvaux (1090–1153), and Ulrich Zwingli (1484–1531), they are good for you, too. One of the things that makes the church a community is the fact that believers pray together.

Since the Lord's Prayer is a family prayer, we not only pray *with* one another, we also pray *for* one another. In the last three petitions we do not pray for ourselves, primarily, but for the whole church.

When we say, "Give us today our daily bread," we are praying for *our daily provision*. We are asking God to meet the material needs of our brothers and sisters. This is why church bulletins often mention who is in the hospital, or what a missionary needs, or which family needs help moving. It is also why small groups spend time sharing personal prayer requests. When Jesus taught us to pray, he taught us to pray for the needs of the family.

Praying for a brother or a sister is one sign of spiritual maturity. Imagine a very demanding little boy. Every day he asks his parents to feed him breakfast, find his shirt, tie his shoes, take him to the park, give him a snack, and do a hundred other things for him. Then one day the boy makes a request, not for himself, but for his little sister. He says, "Dad, can you help my sister? She climbed up on the dresser and can't get down." The boy's father will be touched by his son's concern for another family member. In the same way, our Father in heaven wants us to ask for daily provision for our brothers and sisters.

We are also to pray for *our daily pardon*, which is what we do when we say, "Forgive us our debts." Some sins are private sins. They are committed by an individual within the privacy of the heart. While every Christian needs to confess his or her own personal sins, other sins are corporate sins. They are committed by nations, cities, churches, or families. They may not be anyone's fault in particular, but they are everyone's fault in general. God thus holds us responsible, not only for our individual sins, but also for the sins of our group. That is why so many of the great heroes of the Old Testament—Daniel, for example (Dan. 9:4-19), and Ezra (Ezra 9:5-15)—confessed the sins of the entire nation.

When we pray the Lord's Prayer, we especially confess the corporate sins of the church. What are the prevailing sins of your church? Pride? Envy? Hypocrisy? Prejudice? Greed? These are the kinds of sins that require corporate repentance. As a general rule, the Holy Spirit does not come in his reviving power until a church confesses its sins *as a church*.

Finally, when we say, "Lead us not into temptation, but deliver us from evil," we pray for our *daily protection*.[12] As a pastor, I often offer this kind of prayer on behalf of our congregation: "Some of us will be tempted to sin today, Lord. Keep us from falling! Provide a way of escape! Save us from sin and from Satan!"

Daily provision, daily pardon, daily protection—these are the things we ask for in our family prayer. By praying these things for one another, we strengthen our family ties. As Cyprian once explained:

> Before all things, the Teacher of peace and the Master of unity would not have prayer to be made singly and individually, as for one who prays to pray for himself alone. For we say not "My Father, which art in heaven," nor "Give me this day my daily bread;" nor does each one ask that only his own debt should be forgiven him; nor does he request for himself alone that he may not be led into temptation, and delivered from evil. Our prayer is public and common; and when we pray, we pray not for one, but for the whole people, because we the whole people are one.[13]

PRAY LIKE YOUR BROTHER

There is one final sense in which the Lord's Prayer is a family prayer. It is a prayer we learn from our older Brother.

If we are the children of God, then Jesus Christ is our older Brother. It only makes sense. Since Jesus is God the Son—the unique, eternally-begotten Son of God (John 1:18; 3:16)—God the Father is his Father. But God the Father is also *our* Father, not by divine nature, but by adoption. When we accept the death and resurrection of Jesus Christ for our sins, we become the children of God. Therefore, we share the same Father with Jesus, which makes us his younger brothers and sisters.

This is not only sound logic, it is also the plain teaching of Scripture. According to the writer to the Hebrews, "Both the one who makes men holy and those who are made holy are of the same family" (Heb. 2:11a). "The one who makes men holy," of course, is Jesus himself. He is the one who cleanses us from sin, so that we become holy. The point is that we are in the same family with Jesus. The passage goes on to make this remarkable statement: "So Jesus is not ashamed to call them brothers. He says, 'I will declare your name to my brothers; in the presence of the congregation I will sing your praises'" (Heb. 2:11b-12). Since we have the same Father, and since we belong to the same family, Jesus is not ashamed to be identified as our brother. We are siblings of the Savior.

What does all of this have to do with the Lord's Prayer? It means that Jesus prays the Lord's Prayer with us and for us as our older Brother. When Jesus prayed, "Our Father," he meant *our* Father, the one who is *his* Father as well as *our* Father. Our Father in heaven is also the God and Father of our Lord Jesus Christ. The Lord's Prayer, therefore, is the family prayer we learn from our older Brother.

It has become somewhat fashionable to deny that the Lord's Prayer really is the *Lord's* prayer. Some prefer to call it the "Disciples' Prayer" because, they say, Jesus himself never could have prayed the Lord's Prayer. They point out that it would have been inappropriate for him to use the fifth petition—"Forgive us our debts"—because he did not have any debts to be forgiven. He was the perfect Son of God.

In one sense, it does not matter very much what this prayer is called. Call it the "Lord's Prayer," or the "Disciples' Prayer," or whatever you like. When Jesus taught his disciples the prayer he did not tell them what to call it. But understand that this *is* the Lord's prayer.

That is to say, this is the prayer which Jesus himself prayed through-out his life and ministry. Our elder brother taught us this prayer because it is the way he himself prayed.

Consider how many of these petitions were first uttered by Jesus Christ. "Our Father which art in heaven." This is how Jesus always prayed. Whenever we overhear him praying in the Gospels, he addresses God the Father as "Father." "I praise you, Father, Lord of heaven and earth" (Luke 10:21). "My Father, if it is possible, may this cup be taken from me" (Matt. 26:39). Sometimes he even says, "Holy Father" (John 17:11), which is another way of saying, "Hallowed be thy name."

The petition "Thy will be done, on earth as it is in heaven" was the prayer of Jesus' whole life. "I have come down from heaven not to do my will but to do the will of him who sent me" (John 6:38). Jesus came to do his Father's will on earth, as he had done it in heaven, even when it included suffering and dying for our sins on the cross. In the Garden of Gethsemane, on the eve of the crucifixion, Jesus was "over-whelmed with sorrow to the point of death" (Matt. 26:38). He even asked if the cup of suffering could be taken away from his lips. "Yet," he prayed, "not as I will, but as you will" (Matt. 26:39). In other words, Jesus prayed, "Thy will be done." And God's will *was* done! It was the will of heaven that the Son should die on the cross for our sins. Therefore, when Jesus died on the cross, God's will was done on earth as it had been decreed in heaven.

"Give us this day our daily bread" was Jesus' prayer too. He knew that man does not live on bread alone (Matt. 4:4), yet he still needed to eat his daily bread. Jesus prayed at mealtimes. He looked up to heaven and prayed before he fed the 5,000 (John 6:11). He did the same thing before he gave bread to his disciples at the Last Supper (Matt. 26:26). Jesus did not provide daily bread without first praying for it.

But what about the petition "Forgive us our debts"? It is true that Jesus did not have any debts of his own. Immediately after teaching his disciples to pray, he said, "If you do not forgive men their sins, your Father will not forgive *your* sins" (Matt. 6:15), as if to emphasize that he had no sins of his own. Since he was the perfect Son of God, Jesus

did not commit the least sin. Yet the reason Christ came into the world
was to assume all of our debts upon the cross. "The LORD has laid on
him the iniquity of us all" (Isa. 53:6b). "God made him who had no
sin to be sin for us" (2 Cor. 5:21). When Jesus died on the cross, was
he not asking his Father—at least with his actions, if not with his
words—to forgive us our debts? He was not seeking forgiveness for his
own sins, but for our sins, which he had taken upon himself.
Furthermore, even while he was asking God to forgive our debts, Jesus
forgave his debtors. While they were hurling insults at him, he said,
"Father, forgive them, for they do not know what they are doing"
(Luke 23:34).

Jesus also taught his disciples to say, "And lead us not into temptation, but deliver us from the Evil One." There was a time when Jesus
was led into temptation: "Jesus was led by the Spirit into the desert to
be tempted by the devil" (Matt. 4:1). But once Jesus had resisted those
temptations, he prayed that we would be delivered from Satan, saying
to his Father, "protect them from the Evil One" (John 17:15). Jesus
prayed the same way for Simon Peter, knowing that he would fall
under spiritual attack and deny him three times. Jesus said, "Simon,
Simon, Satan has asked to sift you as wheat. But I have prayed for you,
Simon, that your faith may not fail" (Luke 22:31-32a). Jesus prayed
that his brother Peter would be delivered from the Evil One. In a way,
Jesus offered the same prayer for himself on the cross, when he said,
"Father, into your hands I commit my spirit" (Luke 23:46). Jesus was
praying that his death would not be in vain, that the Father would
deliver him from death and the devil. His prayer was answered when
God raised him from the dead, turning Satan's seeming triumph into
bitter defeat.

Finally, Jesus prayed for God's kingdom, power, and glory. The
kingdom of God is what Jesus came to bring. It is what he preached
and what he promised, perhaps even what he prayed for. He certainly
prayed for God's power and glory: "Father, the time has come. Glorify
your Son, that your Son may glorify you. . . . Holy Father, protect them
by the power of your name" (John 17:1, 11b).

In one way or another, Jesus prayed almost every petition in the

Lord's Prayer. He taught his disciples to pray this way because it was the way *he* prayed. The Lord's Prayer is a "pre-owned prayer." It comes to us secondhand, tried and tested by our Older Brother. And when Jesus made these petitions, his prayers were answered. God's name was hallowed, his kingdom has come, and his will is being done. Through the death and resurrection of Jesus Christ, God the Father forgives our debts and delivers us from the Evil One.

If God has answered the prayers of our Lord, will he not answer us when we pray the Lord's Prayer? To quote again from Cyprian, "how much more effectually do we obtain what we ask in Christ's name, if we ask for it in His own prayer?"[14] If you are a child of God, use your family prayer. Talk to your Father. Pray with your brothers and sisters, the way your older Brother always did. Your Father is ready to listen.

For Discussion

1. Does using a prayer written by someone else help you in your prayer life? What models for prayer have worked well for your own prayer life?

2. How might a model for prayer, such as the Lord's Prayer, help one guard against the ostentatious and repetitive prayers we looked at in chapters 1 and 2?

3. Prayerfully read Matthew 6:9-13. What things do you notice about the general progression or order of the Lord's Prayer?

4. If you think of the Lord's Prayer as a menu for prayer, what titles might you give to each part of the prayer?

5. Why do you think the petitions of the Lord's Prayer are in the order they are? How does each one build on the previous requests in a way that forms a logical progression?

6. What assumptions about God's character are made in these verses?

7. What principles does the Lord's Prayer teach us about effective prayer?

8. Although we learned in chapter 1 that prayer should sometimes be done in secret, the Lord's Prayer is clearly for the whole family of God. What evidence do you see in the prayer itself that supports this premise? Why is it important to pray in the context of the whole family of God?

9. Look at each petition in the Lord's Prayer individually and discuss what is significant about that request being in the plural, rather than singular. For example, by praying for our bread, we are praying not only for our own needs, but for the needs of the hungry throughout the world. The further implication of that prayer is that we should be actively providing for the needs of others before we pray (James 2:14-16).

10. What are some practical ways to pray for and with other Christians? Describe some situations in which you have experienced meaningful prayer with other Christians.

11. Imagine that you are one of the disciples hearing this prayer for the first time. What things about this prayer surprise or impress you?

12. What are some practical ways that the Lord's Prayer can aid a Christian in his or her prayer life even if the words are not quoted word-for-word?

13. If you followed the model of the Lord's Prayer more closely in your own prayer life, how would your prayers change?

4

Our Father in Heaven

Because you are sons, God sent the Spirit of his Son into our hearts, the Spirit who calls out, "Abba, Father."

GALATIANS 4:6

SOME YEARS AGO *Newsweek* magazine ran a story about fatherhood. The point of the article was that fathers—especially God the Father—no longer get the respect they deserve:

> These are tough times to be a father. The media are full of stories about abusive fathers, fatherless children and deadbeat dads. . . . [T]his is an age when fathers get little respect, and you don't have to look farther than the biggest father figure of them all, God. . . .
>
> God the Father is out, unless coupled with God the Mother. . . . Few theologians these days seem to want a God who takes charge, assumes responsibility, fights for his children, makes demands, risks rebuffs, punishes as well as forgives. In a word, a Father.[1]

Theologians may not want a God who takes charge or makes demands, but that is the only God there is. He is who he always has been and always will be. He is our Father.

ABBA, FATHER

The one who taught us the most about the fatherhood of God was God's own Son, who instructed us to pray using these words: "Our Father in heaven" (Matt. 6:9). With these words, Jesus introduced a completely new way to pray. The Jews had always been very careful how they addressed God in their prayers. Some of them had such reverence for God's holiness that they refused to address him by his personal name Yahweh. Nor did Old Testament Scripture directly call him "Father."

The Old Testament does contain the idea of the fatherhood of God. Occasionally, God is referred to as the Father of Israel. Moses asked, "Is he not your Father, your Creator, who made you and formed you?" (Deut. 32:6b; cf. Isa. 63:16).

Yet God is not addressed as "Father" personally and directly in prayer. Kent Hughes writes:

> God is only referred to as Father fourteen times in the huge corpus of the Old Testament's thirty-nine books—and then rather impersonally. In those fourteen occurrences of "Father," the term was always used with reference to the nation, and not individuals. God was spoken of as Israel's Father, but Abraham did not speak of God as "my Father." You can search from Genesis to Malachi, and you will not find such an occurrence.[2]

There is some evidence that by the time of Christ some Jews had begun to pray to God as Father.[3] Eventually, the standard prayers of the synagogue—known as the Eighteen Benedictions—included two petitions that addressed God as "our Father."[4] There were even some pagans, such as the Greeks, who referred to God as the "Father of the living." So Jesus may or may not have been the very first person to pray to God as Father.

Jesus certainly was the first, however, to make the Fatherhood of God so essential to prayer. Jesus calls God "Father" some sixty times in the Gospels. The only exception was his agonizing prayer on the cross, "My God, my God, why have you forsaken me?" (Matt. 27:46). Yet before he breathed his last, Jesus again prayed the way he had always prayed: "Father, into your hands I commit my spirit" (Luke 23:46). Calling God "Father" was the heart of the prayer life of Jesus Christ as it was for no one before him.

Jesus was also the first to use the precise word he chose in addressing his Father. It was the word Jewish children used for their fathers: *abba*. There is an example of this in Mark 14:36, where Jesus prays, "*Abba*, Father." The New Testament was written in Greek, but Jesus himself probably spoke Aramaic. Therefore, it was natural for him to use the word for "father" that he had used while growing up. In fact, *abba* was almost certainly what Jesus called Joseph when he was working in his carpentry shop back in Nazareth.

The word *abba* was picked up by the apostles and used by the first Christians when they prayed. "For you did not receive a spirit that makes you a slave again to fear," wrote Paul to the Romans, "but you received the Spirit of sonship. And by him we cry, '*Abba*, Father'" (Rom. 8:15). The early Christians called God "*Abba*, Father," because that is the way Jesus taught them to pray.

This was a completely new development in the history of prayer. There is no record of anyone else ever having addressed God in such a familiar way. It may have seemed rather presumptuous. Who did Jesus think he was, calling God his Father? Of course Jesus knew exactly who he was—the eternal Son of God. Therefore, he prayed, "*Abba*, Father." He addressed God in a way no one else would dare.

The way Jesus prayed was remarkable. What is more remarkable is that he made it possible for us to pray the same way. First, he made us God's sons and daughters. "To all who received him [Jesus], to those who believed in his name, he [God] gave the right to become children of God" (John 1:12). By trusting in Jesus Christ to save you from sin and death, you are born again as a child of God. You are adopted into God's family.

Until that happens, you cannot properly pray the Lord's Prayer. It is impossible to call God "*Abba*, Father" unless you are a child of God through faith in Jesus Christ. In fact, the early church did not allow visitors to pray the Lord's Prayer until after they had been baptized for the forgiveness of their sins.[5] The Lord's Prayer is for the Lord's disciples. Before you can pray to God as your Father you must first become his true son or daughter through Jesus Christ.

Once you become a child of God, the Holy Spirit enables you to call God your Father. "Because you are sons, God sent the Spirit of his Son into our hearts, the Spirit who calls out, '*Abba*, Father'" (Gal. 4:6).

Every member of the Trinity is involved whenever a Christian utters the word "Father." The Father makes us his children through the Son, and the Spirit enables us to call him our Father. This is a high privilege. "[I]n the Lord's Prayer Jesus authorizes His disciples to repeat the word *abba* after Him. He gives them a share in His sonship and empowers them, as His disciples, to speak with their heavenly Father in just such a familiar, trusting way as a child would with his father."[6]

PRAY WITH CONFIDENCE

How does a child speak to his father? The *Westminster Shorter Catechism* explains this in a wonderful way:

> *Q:* 100. What doth the preface of the Lord's prayer teach us?
> *A:* The preface of the Lord's prayer (which is, *Our Father which art in heaven*) teacheth us to draw near to God with all holy reverence and confidence, as children to a father, able and ready to help us; and that we should pray with and for others.

The catechism understands the heart of a child. Children who love their fathers approach them with *both* the warmest confidence and the deepest reverence. Both of these attitudes are expressed in the Lord's Prayer—confidence and reverence for God the Father.

First, when we pray to God as our Father, we draw near to him with confidence. This confidence comes from intimacy, from knowing that your Father is also your friend.

Sadly, fathers are not always known for intimacy. We are now living in what David Blankenhorn calls *Fatherless America*.[7] Some fathers are absent; they have abandoned their families. Other fathers are weak; they fail to provide spiritual leadership in the home. Still others are emotionally distant; they do not know how to show affection to their families. We have forgotten, perhaps, who a father is and what he does. A real father is a man who has a passionate love for his family. Because of the warmth of his affection—not only for his children, but especially for their mother—his children have the confidence to ask him for what they need.

John Paton, the Scottish missionary to the South Pacific, had confidence in his father's love. When he left his small village on foot to
begin his missionary venture, his father walked with him for the first
few miles. This is the way Paton describes their parting:

> For the last half mile or so we walked on together in almost
> unbroken silence. . . . [My father's] tears fell fast when our eyes
> met each other with looks for which all speech was vain. We
> halted upon reaching the appointed parting place. He grasped
> my hand firmly for a minute in silence and then solemnly and
> affectionately said, "God bless you, my son. Your father's God
> prosper you and keep you from all evil." Unable to say more,
> his lips kept moving in silent prayer. In tears we embraced and
> parted.
>   I ran off as fast as I could and when about to turn a corner
> in the road where he would lose sight of me, I looked back and
> saw him still standing, . . . gazing after me. Waving my hat in
> adieu, I was around the corner and out of sight in an instant,
> but my heart was too full and sore to carry me further, so I
> darted into the side of the road and wept for a time. Then ris-
> ing up cautiously, I climbed the dike to see if he yet stood
> where I left him, and just at that moment I caught a glimpse of
> him climbing the dike and looking out for me. He did not see
> me, and after he had gazed eagerly in my direction for a while,
> he got down, set his face toward home and began to return. . . .
>   I watched through blinding tears till his form faded from my
> gaze, and then hastening on my way, vowed deeply and oft by
> the help of God to live and act so as to never grieve or dishonor
> such a father.[8]

Paton and his father shared a holy affection for one another that
went beyond words. They shared the kind of love Jesus wants us to
experience in God the Father, an intimacy that enables us to approach
him with confidence.

Some people find it difficult to approach God with confidence
because they have never known a father's love. In the providence of
God, they never had a father who blessed them. He may have been

absent or detached and disapproving. Or he was angry and violent. As a result, the last thing they want to do is to give their heart to someone they have to call "Father." In these fatherless times, some people suggest that the language of the Lord's Prayer needs to be amended or abandoned.

The heretical bishop John Shelby Spong has argued that the term "Father" is outdated and offensive. We need to find some other way to address God, he says, a way that avoids the "masculinity of deity" that he finds so repulsive.[9] Yet Jesus teaches us to call God "Father," and to do so with confidence, even if we have never known a father's love. This is because Jesus knows that a father's love is what we have always longed for. He invites us to become God's beloved child. He teaches us to speak to him as our dear Father. That may be difficult at first, but as you learn to pray to God as your Father, you will experience the healing that only the Father's love can bring.

PRAY WITH REVERENCE

Jesus teaches us to pray "*Abba*, Father," so that we will come to God with the confidence of a child. But we do not approach God without reverence. He is our Father in heaven. He dwells in a high and lofty place of majesty, power, and dominion, where he is worshiped by myriads upon myriads of angels. God is so far above us that his exalted position demands our worship and respect.

The fact that God is in heaven does not mean that he is confined by space. God is spirit; he does not have a body. Yet to remind us of his supreme and transcendent greatness, Jesus calls him our Father *in heaven* (Matt. 6:9; cf. 5:45; 23:9). This fact ought to make a great difference when we pray. The philosopher who wrote Ecclesiastes warned:

> *Do not be quick with your mouth,*
> *do not be hasty in your heart*
> *to utter anything before God.*
> *God is in heaven*
> *and you are on earth,*
> *so let your words be few.*
> ECCLESIASTES 5:2

We ought always to approach God with awesome respect. The fact that God is in heaven demands our reverence. But then so does the simple fact that he is our Father. His paternal compassion is reserved for those who give him the respect he deserves. "As a father has compassion on his children, so the LORD has compassion on those who fear him" (Ps. 103:13).

Christians sometimes forget that the Fatherhood of God demands their reverence. It is often said that the best translation of the Aramaic word *abba* is something like "Daddy!" After all, "Daddy" is the word small children use for their fathers in English. If *abba* is the word small children used for their fathers in Aramaic, then "Daddy" it is. As a result, some Christians call God "Daddy" when they pray. I must confess that the idea of calling God "Daddy" has always made me uncomfortable. That is not the way I have addressed my own father for more than twenty years. It suggests immaturity rather than intimacy. Is there not something rather childish about calling God "Daddy"?

At my sister's wedding, my daughter decided to take certain liberties in addressing her father. She was two years old at the time and serving as the flower girl. I was performing the wedding, so I was up at the front of the church. Kirsten was at the back, waiting to come down the aisle. When she looked up, she saw one of her two favorite people in the whole world standing at the front of the church, so in her loudest, most delighted voice, she yelled, "Hi, Dad!" It was a charming moment, but it would not have been quite so charming if Kirsten had been, say, seventeen at the time. Although she spoke to her father with confidence, she did not treat him with reverence.

To call God "*Abba*, Father" is to speak to him with reverence as well as confidence. *Abba* does not mean "Daddy." To prove this point, the Oxford linguist James Barr wrote an article for the *Journal of Theological Studies* called "Abba Isn't 'Daddy.'"[10] What Barr discovered was that *abba* was not merely a word used by young children. It was also the word that Jewish children used for their parents after they were fully grown. *Abba* was a mature, yet affectionate way for adults to speak to their fathers.[11]

The New Testament is careful not to be too casual in the way it addresses God. The Aramaic word *abba* appears three times in the New Testament (Mark 14:36; Rom. 8:15; Gal. 4:6). In each case, it is followed immediately by the Greek word *pater. Pater* is not the Greek word for "Daddy." The Greek language has a word for "Daddy"—the word *pappas*—but that is not the word the New Testament uses to translate *abba.* Instead, in order to make sure that our intimacy with God does not become an excuse for immaturity, it says, "*abba, pater.*"

The best way to translate *abba* is "Dear Father," or even "Dearest Father." That phrase captures both the warm confidence and the deep reverence that we have for our Father in heaven. It expresses our intimacy with God, while still preserving his dignity. When we pray, therefore, we are to say, "Our dear Father in heaven." The Dutch Bible scholar Herman Ridderbos concludes: "This address lends a twofold character to the entire prayer. On the one hand it pervades it with a childlike trust ('Our Father'), on the other hand, with reverence and an awareness of distance ('in heaven'). Such a frame of mind grants God the honor that is His due and grants the person praying the certainty that he will be heard."[12]

WHAT ARE FATHERS FOR?

We come to God with both reverence and confidence. But what do we come for? We come for what children usually come to their fathers for. In the last petitions of the Lord's Prayer, we ask for exactly the kinds of things that children ask for from their fathers: provision, pardon, and protection.

First, we pray for *provision.* We beg God, "Give us today our daily bread." Providing daily bread is part of a father's job. He is the breadwinner. It's a compliment to be called a "good provider." God the Father is not only a good provider, he is the best provider of all. Jesus once told a short story about God's ability to provide. The story began with a couple of rhetorical questions: "Which of you, if his son asks for bread, will give him a stone? Or if he asks for a fish, will give him a snake?" (Matt. 7:9-10).

To understand these questions, imagine the following scene: Johnny is celebrating his sixth birthday. There will be a party with balloons, streamers, cake, candles, and best of all, presents! Johnny can hardly wait. For weeks he has been dropping hints about what kind of present he would like best. He has been none too subtle about it, either. His hints have been more like demands. He wants a new bike.

The big day finally arrives. The guests arrive, and sure enough, his father gives him a large box, wrapped in shiny paper and festooned with ribbons. Johnny tears off the wrapping paper, opens the box, and finds . . . a sack of gravel. It is such a bitter disappointment that the poor boy bursts into tears. Then it is time to eat, so Johnny cheers up a bit. His father brings out a silver platter covered with a silver dome and sets it in the middle of the table. With a grand flourish, he whips off the dome and a cloud of steam rises from the platter. As the steam clears, Johnny sees a slimy snake slithering towards him across the table.

The whole scene is unimaginable. Even the worst of fathers knows how to give his son a nice birthday present, which is exactly the point Jesus was trying to make: "If you, then, though you are evil, know how to give good gifts to your children, how much more will your Father in heaven give good gifts to those who ask him!" (Matt. 7:11). God will provide everything we need to live because he is our gracious heavenly Father.

Second, we ask our Father for *pardon*. We pray, "Forgive us our debts, as we also have forgiven our debtors" (Matt. 6:12). Granting pardon is also part of a father's job. When children are naughty, they usually have to answer to their fathers.

I remember a time when I had to answer to my father. It was long after I was old enough to know better, but I had told a lie. Worse, I had implicated my father in the lie. Worst of all (for me), I got caught. As ashamed as I was, I still went to my father to confess my sin. I knew that he would forgive me. He had to forgive me, because I will always be his son.

Jesus once told a story about a son who returned to his father to ask for pardon (Luke 15:11-32). The son was sick and tired of living at home with his father, so he ran away to spend his fortune. For a while he had the time of his life. But once his line of credit ran out, and he could no longer maintain the lifestyle to which he had grown accustomed, all his "friends" left him. Homeless and hungry, and not quite on the career trajectory he had been expecting, the young man managed to get a job slopping hogs. While he was wallowing in the muck he finally came to his senses. He remembered how well his father had provided for him. Then he realized there was still a chance his father might pardon him.

Hoping for pardon, the son went back home. While he was still a long way off, his father recognized him and ran to meet him. The father threw his arms around his son, kissed him, and then called for feasting and dancing. The son was forgiven for all his sins.

This story is about the prodigal God who squanders his love on a rebellious son. But the key to the whole story is the first word out of the son's mouth: "Father." "The son said to him, 'Father, I have sinned against heaven and against you'" (Luke 15:21a). What gave the son the confidence to go home and seek pardon for his sins was that he was going home to his father.

In much the same way, it is the Fatherhood of God that gives us the confidence to ask God to pardon our sins. Like the wayward son, we say, "Father, I have sinned against you." This is part of the logic of the Lord's Prayer. We would never have the courage to ask God to forgive us our debts (in the fifth petition) unless we already knew that we could call him our Father (from the preface). The reason we pray to God as our Father—and the reason our Father will forgive us—is because Jesus has paid for our sins through his death on the cross.

Finally, we pray for *protection*. We ask our Father to "lead us not into temptation, but deliver us from the Evil One" (Matt. 6:13). In making this petition, we are asking God to defend us from sin and from Satan. Defending the family is another part of a father's responsibility. He is a protector as well as a provider.

I was reminded of a father's responsibility to protect his family during a violent thunderstorm. Lightning was flashing on every side, followed instantaneously by the sound of thunder. The storm cell passed right over our house. In fact, two of the houses on our street were struck by lightning. Frankly, I was scared (probably more scared than my wife was) but not too scared to realize that my children might be scared, too. So I ran upstairs, scooped my son out bed, and carried him down to the basement.

That is what fathers do—they protect their children. God the Father is no exception. He is our shelter in the time of storm. He is the one who lifts us up with strong arms in the day of trouble and carries us to a safe place. Therefore, he is the Father to whom we pray.

If you are God's child, then the reality of God's fatherly care ought to dominate not only your prayers, but also your whole outlook on life. J. I. Packer has wisely written:

> If you want to judge how well a person understands Christianity, find out how much he makes of the thought of being God's child, and having God as his father. If this is not the thought that prompts and controls his worship and prayers and his whole outlook on life, it means that he does not understand Christianity very well at all. For everything that Christ taught . . . is summed up in the knowledge of the Fatherhood of God.[13]

Packer is right. Everything you really need—provision, pardon, protection—depends on the Fatherhood of God. God is your loving Father, so he is willing to help you. He is your Father in heaven, with infinite resources at his disposal, so he is also able to help you. Now Jesus invites you to draw near to God, confidently and reverently, asking him for what you need, and calling him, "Dearest Father."

For Discussion

1. What images of fathers are prevalent in contemporary culture? Choose a father from a movie or TV show as an example of how many people view fathers.

2. How do negative images of fathers impact how both Christians and non-Christians view God?

3. When Jesus taught his disciples to pray, he started out by giving them

a specific way to address him. Read Matthew 6:9 to find out what he said. If you were a Jew in Jesus' day, what would your reaction be to Jesus calling God "Father"?

4. What principles can you infer from this verse about how we should approach God?

5. Do you feel comfortable addressing God as Father? What hesitations (if any) do you have about thinking of God in this way?

6. In trying to balance our confidence before God with our reverence for him, which way do you think the contemporary church usually errs? Why do you think that is?

7. Which way do you personally tend to err?

8. What are some practical ways to balance intimacy and reverence in your relationship with God?

9. Think of an image or story that illustrates what a good father is like. What kinds of things does a good father do for his children?

10. The Bible tells us that God is our Father. Read Matthew 7:7-11 to learn more about what a good father is like. In your own words, tell what believers are encouraged to do in verse 7.

11. Some people interpret verse 8 to mean that if your prayers are not answered, you have not asked properly, lack faith, or are not persistent enough. How would you respond to that argument in light of 1 John 5:14-15 and Ephesians 6:18?

12. What does Matthew 7:7-11 tell us about the type of father God is?

13. Is the picture of God given in this passage hard for you to accept? Why or why not?

14. Think back to how you answered question 9 above. If good earthly fathers do the things you mentioned, what kinds of things are

included in the "how much more will God give good gifts to those who ask him" of Matthew 7:11?

15. Take a moment to share with the group one or two gifts that God has given you in response to your prayers.

16. How should the fact that God is the kind of Father pictured in this passage affect our prayers? Our day-to-day lives?

17. What things are there in your life right now that you either have been praying consistently for or are encouraged, after studying this passage, to begin asking for? Claim God's promises in verses 7-8 to answer your prayers. Pray boldly for the things that are on your heart.

5

Holy Is Your Name

Holy and awesome is his name.
PSALM 111:9b

I HAVE NEVER SEEN anyone struck dead during a worship service. Ever. This may or may not surprise you, but it sometimes surprises me. To tell the truth, I am surprised that *I* haven't been struck with a thunderbolt during a worship service. I often get distracted while I worship. My mind wanders from things that are heavenly and eternal to things that are earthly and mundane. At times my affections are cold, my thoughts carnal. Most of my worship, if not quite all of it, is unworthy of the God who is majestic in his holiness.

I assume that other people experience similar distractions when they worship. They stand up to sing and close their eyes to pray, but what are they really thinking? And who are they really worshiping? I suspect that most people would be embarrassed to admit what goes through their minds and hearts during public worship. That is why I say that I am surprised that I have never seen anyone struck dead during a church service.

It has happened before. One minute people were worshiping and the next minute they were dead. It happened to Nadab and Abihu, the sons of Aaron. While they were serving as priests at the tabernacle they offered unholy fire, contrary to God's command. "So fire came out from the presence of the LORD and consumed them, and they died before the LORD" (Lev. 10:2). Much the same thing happened to Uzzah. God's people were moving the ark of God's presence to Jerusalem on an ox cart. When the oxen stumbled, Uzzah thought God needed his help, so he reached out his hand to steady the ark. "The LORD's anger burned against Uzzah, and he struck him down because he had put his hand on the ark. So he died there before God" (1 Chron. 13:10).

What we learn from these examples is that it is not altogether safe to come into the presence of a holy God. Consider the epitaph God wrote for Nadab and Abihu after they were incinerated: "Among those who approach me I will show myself holy" (Lev. 10:3a). On occasion, God has shown himself to be holy by striking down people who offer him unholy worship. Until we recognize the inherent danger of coming into God's presence, we have not really begun to worship him in the purity of his holiness. God is not a warm glow, like the dying embers on the hearth. He is a consuming fire.

THE HOLY ONE

The Lord's Prayer compels us to acknowledge God's bright and burning holiness. From the very beginning, it directs our thoughts towards God and his perfections. First comes the address, in which we cry to our Father in heaven. Yet lest we approach him too casually, the first petition reminds us that he is a holy Father: "Hallowed be your name." As we begin the asking part of our prayer, then, the first thing we beg God to do is to make his name to be holy.

Now to make this petition properly we must understand what it means to be holy, what God's name is, and how God makes that name holy. To be holy is to be set apart in purity. It is to be separated from what is common and ordinary in order to be devoted to God's service. Whatever is holy is distinguished from the secular and dedicated to the sacred.

Many things were hallowed (or sanctified) this way in the Old Testament. The children of Israel were set apart from the other nations for God's holy service. The Levites were set apart from the other tribes to offer holy worship in God's house. The tabernacle was set apart from all the other tents in the camp for God's holy presence. Within the tabernacle, the Holy of Holies was "set apart and awe-inspiring in an almost physical way so as to be dangerous to the trespasser over the boundary into the holy."[1] For the people of God, holiness was not just for the Sabbath, it was part of daily life. Throughout the Old

Testament, a distinction is made between clean and unclean. Certain foods, garments, and utensils were clean, while others were unclean. This did not have to do with hygiene, it had to do with holiness. As far as the Jews were concerned, cleanliness was next to holiness.

If to be holy is to be set apart in purity, then how holy must God be? "There is no one holy like the LORD" (1 Sam. 2:2a). No one is more un-common and extra-ordinary than he is, which explains why the biblical word used to describe him more than any other is the word "holy."[2] God is other. He alone is immortal and lives in unapproachable light (1 Tim. 6:16). There is a vast and infinite distance between the Creator and the creature. As high as the heavens are above the earth, so high is his holiness.

Even the angels in heaven, as pure and as perfect as they are, recognize that God is set apart from them. When the prophet Isaiah entered the throne room of heaven, he saw the Lord high and lifted up. He heard the seraphim, the "burning ones," calling out to one another, "Holy, holy, holy is the LORD Almighty; the whole earth is full of his glory" (Isa. 6:3). All the while, the angels kept themselves separate from the Most Holy One. "With two wings they covered their faces, and with two they covered their feet" (Isa. 6:2), thus setting God apart in his unique purity.

When we say that God is holy we do not simply mean that he does not sin. That is true, of course. God's holiness has an ethical dimension. The Bible says that "the holy God will show himself holy by his righteousness" (Isa. 5:16b). God is undefiled in all his ways. He is the supreme, the superlative moral majesty in the universe. But God's holiness refers to more than his ethics. Holiness refers to everything that distinguishes the Creator from his creation. It is the infinite distance between his deity and our humanity. Holiness is the very "Godness" of God, the sum total of all his glorious perfections.

WHAT'S IN A NAME?

Because God is so holy, everything associated with him is holy. His law is holy, and so is his promise. His ways, his words, his works, and his wrath are holy. His priests are holy. Even his people are holy, in the sense that we are set apart for his service. God says, "You are to be holy to me because I, the LORD, am holy, and I have set you apart from the nations to be my own" (Lev. 20:26). But perhaps the best way to take the various aspects of God's holiness and bring them all together in one place is to say that God's *name* is holy (Ps. 103:1; 111:9).

These days most people think names are relatively unimportant. "What's in a name?" Romeo asked Juliet. "That which we call a rose / By any any other word would smell as sweet."[3] In other words, a name is just a name, and there isn't much in it. A rose by any other name might smell as sweet, but if it had another name, Shakespeare would not have written about it! Notice that Romeo did not try to tell Juliet that "a flowering cactus by any other name would smell as sweet." It takes the right name to convey the essence of the thing.

This is why the Old Testament people of God took names as seriously as they did. They did not name their children after sports figures, soap opera stars, or Disney characters. They gave them names that would reflect the essence of their divine calling. They understood that a name is not a label, it is an identity. People do not just *have* names, they *are* their names.

This is especially true when it comes to the holy name of God. God's name expresses his person; it reflects who he is. The name is God himself, as he has made himself known. It reveals his divine nature and his eternal qualities. God is who his name is. Thus all the biblical names and titles for God reveal his true character. Most of them refer to one of his actions or attributes. He is Jehovah-Jireh, the God who provides. He is El-Shaddai, the Mighty God. He is the Holy One, the Everlasting Father. He is the Maker and the Redeemer. He is the Shepherd, the Rock, and the Hiding Place. Whatever the name, God is who his name is because he does what his name says.

There is one name for God, however, that does not refer to any one of his actions or attributes. It is also the name by which he is called more than any other, the name which appears nearly 7,000 times in the Old Testament. It is the name Yahweh, or Jehovah, written in most English translations as "LORD," in all capital letters. Yahweh is the special name God revealed to Moses at the burning bush. God had a job for Moses to do, which he was willing to do, but first he wanted to know God's name so he could tell the people who his boss was. God said to Moses, "I AM WHO I AM. This is what you are to say to the Israelites: 'I AM has sent me to you'" (Exod. 3:14). The name God gave to Moses meant that God is who he is. He is self-existent, self-sufficient, and self-sustaining. He is the eternal Lord of all that is, all that was, and all that will ever be.

Yahweh, Jehovah, the Great I AM, or the LORD—this special name is the summary of everything God has revealed about himself. It stands for all his divine attributes and represents his entire reputation. Thus the great Jewish theologian Moses Maimonides (1135–1204) said: "All the names of God which occur in Scripture are derived from His works except one, and that is Jehovah; and this is called the plain name, because it teaches plainly and unequivocally of the substance of God."[4] "LORD" is the special name God has chosen to hallow. ". . . Revere this glorious and awesome name—the LORD your God" (Deut. 28:58b). In response, we say with the prophet Jeremiah, "No one is like you, O LORD; you are great, and your name is mighty in power" (Jer. 10:6). Or we sing with King David, "O LORD, our LORD, how majestic is your name in all the earth!" (Ps. 8:1a). Or we shout with the seraphim, "Holy, holy, holy is the LORD Almighty; the whole earth is full of his glory" (Isa. 6:3).

SANCTIFY YOUR NAME

We are starting to understand what Jesus meant when he taught us to pray, "Hallowed be your name." What does it mean to be holy? To be holy is to be set apart in purity. What is God's name? God's name, especially the name "Yahweh," is the sum total of his character. But what does it mean for God's name to be hallowed?

Hallowing God's name does not mean that God can become any more holy than he is. God is already "majestic in holiness" (Exod. 15:11). He is as perfectly holy as he can possibly be. Therefore, when we ask God to hallow his name, we cannot ask him to be anything more than he already is. Yet the first petition of the Lord's Prayer *is* a petition. It does ask for something. When we pray, "Hallowed be your name," we are not simply claiming that God is holy. This is more than a statement, it is a request. We are imploring God to *do* something.

What we are asking God to do in the first petition is to satisfy his own chief end, which is to glorify himself. God is hallowed whenever he shows that he is the Holy One. When we ask him to hallow his name, therefore, all we are doing is asking him to reveal that he is exactly who he is. Since God is holy, and his name is holy, to ask God to make his name holy is simply to ask him to live up to his name. It is an appeal for God to reveal himself as he actually is, a request for God to offer a glimpse of his hidden holiness. "Hallowed be your name" means "Make yourself known as the Holy One that you are." It is a prayer for God to display the God-ness of his Godhood.

In particular, in the first petition of the Lord's Prayer, we are asking God's name to be hallowed by ourselves and by other human beings. Augustine commented, "This is prayed for, not as if the name of God were not holy already, but that it may be held holy by men."[5] The petition thus has an evangelistic purpose. It echoes one of the prayers of Asaph in the Psalms: "Let them know that you, whose name is the LORD—that you alone are the Most High over all the earth" (Ps. 83:18). God's name is hallowed when human beings declare that he is holy, and thus give him the honor he deserves. What better way to begin our prayers? When we get on our knees, the first thing we ask of God is to glorify himself, to show that he is utterly transcendent in his holiness. We pray that God would be given that unique reverence that his nature and character demand.[6]

The story is told of a wise and benevolent king who was loved and honored by all his subjects. One morning each week he opened his throne room to the general public. On that morning he would hear grievances and listen to petitions, making himself available to meet the needs of his people. There was one man who faithfully came to see the king week after week. Yet he never bothered the king with a single complaint or request. He simply stood at the back of the throne room. After a while this began to puzzle the king. Who was this man who came every week? And why did he come, if not to ask for help?

One day the king summoned the man to approach his throne and inquired after his business. "Your majesty," the man said, "when I was a young man I committed a crime and I was sentenced to death. Yet as I was dragged through the streets to the gallows, I saw you riding on your horse and I cried out for mercy. Since I was such a young man you granted me a royal pardon and commanded me to be released. That is why I come to stand in your presence every week. I do not come to ask for anything. What more could I ask for? You have already given me my life and my freedom. I come only to pay you homage, to honor you as your devoted servant."[7]

We do the same thing when we pray the Lord's Prayer. We are entering the throne room of our gracious King. There will be time for the rest of our petitions in due course. But we must begin by paying homage to our heavenly Father, the King. First we offer him all the awe and reverence that he alone deserves, praising him and adoring him in the beauty of his holiness.

A HOLY SACRIFICE

In order for us to come into God's holy presence something has to be done about our sin. That is the way it was for the man who went to see the king. Before he could come and stand in the palace, he had to be saved from the punishment he deserved for his crimes. The same thing is true, of course, in our relationship with God. Of all the things that separate us from our great King, it is our sin that creates the greatest distance.

King David asked, "Who may ascend the hill of the LORD? Who may stand in his holy place?" (Ps. 24:3). His answer was, "He who has clean hands and a pure heart" (Ps. 24:4a). But this is exactly our problem. We have filthy hands and impure hearts. We are as unholy as God is holy. Therefore, we find ourselves keeping our distance, standing at the bottom of the hill, not daring to ascend and meet with God in his holy place. We are like the children of Israel at Sinai, where they were told not to touch the mountain, lest they die (Exod. 19:12-13).

The problem of sin explains why anyone who has ever encountered God in all his holiness has at first been filled with utter despair. The prophet Isaiah is a good example. When Isaiah went to heaven and saw God worshiped in all his holiness, it did not inspire him, it terrified him. He cried out, "Woe to me! . . . I am ruined! For I am a man of unclean lips, and I live among a people of unclean lips, and my eyes have seen the King, the LORD Almighty" (Isa. 6:5). Isaiah thought he was a dead man. He was too unholy to worship a holy, holy, holy God. But God did something about Isaiah's sin. One of the angels took a coal from the altar of sacrifice and touched it to Isaiah's lips. He said, "See, this has touched your lips; your guilt is taken away and your sin atoned for" (Isa. 6:7). Then and only then could Isaiah worship God in his holiness. Before he could begin to hallow God properly, his sins had to be forgiven, and that could only be done on the basis of a sacrifice.

Our own situation is no different. We are as unholy as Isaiah was. We cannot hallow God until God hallows us, which he does through his Son Jesus Christ, the Holy One of God. Jesus came to this earth to give his life as a holy sacrifice for sin. As the time of his crucifixion drew near he said, "Now my heart is troubled, and what shall I say? 'Father, save me from this hour'? No, it was for this very reason I came to this hour. Father, glorify your name!" (John 12:27-28a). Jesus died on the cross to glorify his Father's name. In other words, the way Jesus hallowed God's name was by suffering and dying for our sins.

Once it was God's holiness that separated us from God, the holiness of his being. Now it is God's holiness that brings us to God, the holiness of the perfect sacrifice Jesus offered for our sins on the cross. God displayed his holiness by making us holy through his holy Son.

A HOLY LIFE

If Christ died to make us holy, then holy we must be. Consider the surprising word the New Testament uses over and over to describe God's people. The word is "saint," which means "holy one." It is significant that the Greek noun for "saint" comes from the same root as the Greek verb "to hallow."

This means that one of the places God hallows himself is in us. He answers the first petition of the Lord's Prayer by "sanctifying" his "saints," or "hallowing" his "holy ones." In one of the oldest commentaries on this prayer, Cyprian observed that we pray "not that we wish for God that He may be hallowed by our prayers, but that we beseech of Him that His name may be hallowed in us."[8]

God begins to make his name holy in us at baptism. Christians are baptized, after all, in the *name* of the Father, the Son, and the Holy Spirit (Matt. 28:19). Not only are we baptized into this name, we are also sanctified by it. "You were washed, you were sanctified, you were justified in the name of the Lord Jesus Christ and by the Spirit of our God" (1 Cor. 6:11). Now that God has placed his name on us, he is known to be holy whenever we are holy. The Scripture thus gives us this command: "Let him who is holy continue to be holy" (Rev. 22:11). If you bear the name "Christian," you must be what you are: set apart for God in purity. You *are* holy because of what Jesus Christ has done *for* you. But you must continue to *be* holy by what his Spirit does *in* you.

In his *Large Catechism*, Luther asked when God's name would be hallowed among us. His answer was, "When both our teaching and our life are godly and Christian."[9] And the only way to obtain a truly Christian life is to pray for it.

So ask God to make you holy in your actions. Do not use the parts of your body to do what is immoral or shameful. Instead, use your feet to spread the Gospel, your hands to feed the poor, and your arms to lift up the weak.

Ask God to make you holy in your words. Do not curse or use coarse language. The reason this kind of talk is called "profanity" is because it profanes God's name (see Lev. 22:31-32). Obviously the first petition of the Lord's Prayer is closely related to the third commandment: "You shall not misuse the name of the LORD your God, for the LORD will not hold anyone guiltless who misuses his name" (Exod. 20:7). Instead of cursing, use your mouth for blessing. And when you speak about spiritual things do it reverently, not with words that merely sound pious, but with genuine piety.

Ask God to make you holy in your thoughts. Do not fill your mind with things that are violent. Do not indulge in sexual fantasy. Instead, use your mind to contemplate the holiness of God and the purity of everything he has made. "Whatever is true, whatever is noble, whatever is right, whatever is pure, whatever is lovely, whatever is admirable—if anything is excellent or praiseworthy—think about such things" (Phil. 4:8).

Ask God to make you holy in your emotions. To put it negatively, put away your unrighteous anger and your self-pity. To put it positively, put on the emotions of Jesus Christ. Love the things he loves. Hate the things he hates. Be brokenhearted for the things that break his heart. Holy emotions were one of the shining characteristics of Henry Martyn (1781–1812), the Cambridge scholar who traveled as a missionary to India and translated the Bible into Persian. At one point in his travels, Martyn saw a drawing in which Jesus was portrayed catching hold of the garments of Mohammed and bowing down to worship him. Martyn was so deeply distressed by the picture that he burst into tears. When someone asked him what was the matter he said, "I could not endure existence if Jesus were not to be glorified. It would be hell to me if he were always thus to be dishonored."[10] Martyn was a holy man, for even his emotions were shaped by the holiness of God.

Ask God to make you holy in your worship. When we worship God properly, we leave off seeking a name for ourselves and begin to seek the honor of his name. We make known to ourselves and to others that God's name is holy. Therefore, do not just go through the motions when you go to church. Instead, worship God reverently, with a proper sense of *who he is*. Worship with a holy and devoted heart, praising him with everything you have. "Ascribe to the LORD the glory due his name" (Ps. 96:8).

To summarize, pray that God would make you holy in everything you do, say, think, feel, and adore. "Just as he who called you is holy, so be holy in all you do; for it is written: 'Be holy, because I am holy'" (1 Pet. 1:15). This is the whole task of the Christian life: to become what God is in his holiness. In other words, to hallow his name.

Happily, this is a prayer God intends to answer. His plan is to reveal more and more of his perfection until the whole earth is full of his holiness. "From the west, men will fear the name of the LORD, and from the rising of the sun, they will revere his glory" (Isa. 59:19). As the *Westminster Shorter Catechism* states, "In the first petition (which is, *Hallowed be thy name*) we pray, That God would enable us and others to glorify him in all that whereby he maketh himself known; and that he would dispose all things to his own glory" (A. 101).

The Puritan Thomas Watson (d. c. 1690) had a beautiful thought about this prayer. His thought was that "hallowed be your name" is the one petition that God's people will continue to make for all eternity.

> When some of the other petitions shall be useless and out of date, as we shall not need to pray in heaven, 'Give us our daily bread,' because there shall be no sin; nor, 'Lead us not into temptation,' because the old serpent is not there to tempt: yet the hallowing of God's name will be of great use and request in heaven; we shall be ever singing hallelujahs, which is nothing else but the hallowing of God's name.[11]

We will join with the voices of angels, who never stop saying, "Holy, holy, holy is the Lord God Almighty, who was, and is, and is to come" (Rev. 4:8b).

For Discussion

1. The first thing we are to do when we begin the petitionary part of our prayer is to beg God to make his name holy. The Bible often speaks of holiness. What do you think this term means?

2. Share an experience that helped you understand God's holiness or your own unholiness.

3. Perhaps the best place in the Bible to understand God's holiness in contrast with the unholiness of humanity is Isaiah 6. Turn there and read verses 1-8. What does Isaiah's vision in verses 1-4 reveal about the nature of God's holiness?

4. How did Isaiah respond to seeing God's holiness? Have you ever been so aware of God's holiness that you reacted in a similar way?

5. What do you think Isaiah meant when he confessed living "among a people of unclean lips"? Why did he consider that a sin?

6. What caused Isaiah to move from a paralyzing sense of his own unholiness to a bold willingness to answer God's call in verse 8? What is the theological significance of the coal that was brought from God's altar to Isaiah's lips?

7. Isaiah spent the rest of his life calling people to revere the Lord. Read Isaiah 45:1-8 and discuss what this passage adds to your understanding of God's holiness.

8. Based on this text alone, what methods does God use to make us holy?

9. Discuss your answer to the previous question in light of what you know about sanctification from the rest of the Bible. Read James 1:2-4 and Romans 6:5-7 for a few ideas.

10. What are some names of God that we find in the Bible? What does each name teach us about God?

11. All of God's names are derived from his works (Creator, Provider, Mighty God) except one: "Yahweh," or Jehovah. That is the name God has chosen to hallow, and the name that teaches plainly and completely the substance of God. What are we asking for when we ask, as the Lord's Prayer does, for God to hallow his name?

12. Read Psalm 83:18 and Deuteronomy 28:58. How do these verses expand your understanding of the first petition of the Lord's Prayer?

13. God's name is hallowed when human beings declare that he is holy, and thus give him the honor he deserves. Read the following verses and discuss the specific ways we can hallow God's name in our lives: Romans 12:1-2; Exodus 20:7; Philippians 4:8; Proverbs 8:13.

14. What step are you ready to take toward hallowing God's name in your life?

15. What aspect of your prayer life do you want to change as a result of this study on hallowing God's holy name?

6

Your Kingdom Come

The kingdom of God has come upon you.
MATTHEW 12:28b

SOMETIMES IT IS HARD to believe God's kingdom will ever come. The world is troubled by poverty, injustice, and war. The Gospel seems to make little progress from one day to the next. The wicked triumph while the righteous go about in chains. When we see all this we do not stop praying for the kingdom, but we do want to ask God, "When will your kingdom come?"

The German theologian Helmut Thielicke wrestled with this question at the end of World War II. In 1945 he stood in the ruins of the University Chapel in Hamburg, preaching on the Lord's Prayer. This is what Thielicke said about the coming of the kingdom:

> We must not think of it as a gradual Christianization of the world which will increasingly eliminate evil. Such dreams and delusions, which may have been plausible enough in more peaceful times, have vanished in the terrors of our man-made misery. . . . Who can still believe today that we are developing toward a state in which the kingdom of God reigns in the world of nations, in culture, and in the life of the individual? The earth has been plowed too deep by the curse of war, the streams of blood and tears have swollen all too terribly, injustice and bestiality have become all too cruel and obvious for us to consider such dreams to be anything but bubbles and froth.[1]

In the aftermath of the battered, bloody end of the twentieth century, we can add further stanzas to Thielicke's lament. When, if ever, will God's kingdom come?

TWO KINGDOMS IN CONFLICT

To understand the slow coming of God's kingdom, it helps to remember that almost from the very beginning, there have really been two kingdoms. Augustine wrote about them in his great work *The City of God*. He said there are two kingdoms: the kingdom of God and the kingdom of man. Each of these two kingdoms has its own ruler, its own people, its own desire, and its own destiny.

The kingdom of God is ruled by Almighty God, and its people are his loyal subjects. Their heart's desire is for God himself and for his glory. The ultimate destiny of that kingdom is to rule on earth as it does in heaven. Yet over against God's kingdom stands the kingdom of this world, ruled by Satan. Its subjects are men and women in rebellion against God. They love only themselves, to the contempt of their Creator. Thus their evil kingdom is destined to fail. One day it will be swallowed up in the victory of God. But in the meantime, Satan and his followers battle God's kingdom at every turn.

The battle was engaged in the Garden of Eden. There the Lord God placed the man and the woman he had created. He commanded them to be fruitful, to multiply, and to subdue the earth. In other words, God wanted Adam and Eve to establish his kingdom. But Satan would not stand for it. He persuaded first the woman and then the man to strive for their own glory rather than to seek for God's kingdom. The rest of human history has been the story of these two kingdoms in conflict: the kingdom of man and the kingdom of God.

Consider the history of God's people Israel. Through Abraham, Isaac, and Jacob, God set apart a people for himself. Satan conspired to enslave them in Egypt under the dominion of his Pharaoh. After 400 long years God delivered his people from that evil kingdom. He led them into the promised land, where he established a kingdom for his own people.

For a time, God's people were content to have God for their only king. Israel was led by men like Gideon, who said, "I will not rule over you, nor will my son rule over you. The LORD will rule over you" (Judges 8:23). But the day came when the people decided to seek their own kingdom rather than to submit to God's kingship. "We want a king over us," they said. "Then we will be like all the other nations, with a king to lead us and to go out before us and fight our battles" (1 Sam. 8:19b-20). God gave his people what they wanted, but not before warning them that one day their kings would rebel against his kingdom. There were some good kings, of course. There were men like David, who said, "Yours, O LORD, is the kingdom" (1 Chron. 29:11). But eventually the kings of Israel forgot who the real King was, and their kingdom was taken away from them. God's people were carried off by Assyria and Babylon, kingdoms of this world. And though after many years of exile they returned, they never regained the glory of their kingdom.

God's people never stopped longing for the kingdom, however. This longing is expressed in prayers from the post-exilic period, like these petitions from the Kaddish: "Magnified and sanctified be his great name in the world which he hath created according to his will. May he establish his kingdom during your life and during your days."[2] The Old Testament closes with God's people waiting . . . waiting and wondering when their king will come.

THE COMING OF THE KING

Then the king came. He was born in the royal city of Bethlehem, born to reign on David's throne, born the king of the Jews. They called him Jesus, the Christ. Yet no sooner was he born than Satan tried to kill him. Herod sent soldiers to search and destroy every male child in Bethlehem. The king of this world tried to kill God's King while he was still in the cradle.

God saved his newborn King and kept him safe until he became a man. Then Satan tried to destroy him again. Jesus went out into the wilderness to be tempted by the devil. Having failed at murder, Satan attempted bribery. And what did he have to offer? A kingdom. "The devil led him up to a high place and showed him in an instant all the kingdoms of the world. And he said to him, 'I will give you all their authority and splendor, for it has been given to me, and I can give it to anyone I want to. So if you worship me, it will all be yours'" (Luke 4:5-7). Satan was trying to get Jesus to abdicate his throne. The temptation was to trade the kingdom of God for the kingdom of this world. But Jesus rejected Satan's offer because he wanted to be God's King, not Satan's king.

Immediately afterwards, Jesus began his kingly ministry. "From that time on Jesus began to preach, 'Repent, for the kingdom of heaven is near'"(Matt. 4:17). Those were the very first words of his public ministry. With them Jesus announced the major theme of the Gospels: the coming of the kingdom. Jesus is the King, and the coming of the King means the coming of the kingdom, which Jesus mentioned more than 100 times in the New Testament. Jesus not only began his ministry with the kingdom, but he also ended it that way. After his resurrection, before he ascended into heaven, he continued to teach his disciples. And what did he teach them? "He appeared to them over a period of forty days and spoke about the kingdom of God" (Acts 1:3b). From beginning to end, the Gospel according to Jesus is the good news about God's kingdom.

In one sense, of course, God has always been the King. "The LORD has established his throne in heaven, and his kingdom rules over all" (Ps. 103:19). "His dominion is an eternal dominion; his kingdom endures from generation to generation" (Dan. 4:34b). This universe has never been a democracy; it has always been an absolute monarchy, for God has always been on the throne.

Yet God's kingship has also been a matter of endless dispute. God has always had to fight to defend his sovereign rule against the kingdom of darkness. Even now an invisible war rages between God and Satan for the souls of men and women. We see the casualties all around: abuse, addiction, hatred, injustice, and war. No wonder it takes so long for the kingdom to come! There are two kingdoms, not one, and God's kingdom cannot come without Satan's kingdom being destroyed.

It takes a king to establish a kingdom, which is why God sent Jesus into the world. "The reason the Son of God appeared was to destroy the devil's work" (1 John 3:8b). And destroy it he did. He not only preached the kingdom, he practiced it. "Jesus went throughout Galilee teaching in their synagogues, preaching the good news of the kingdom, and healing every disease and sickness among the people" (Matt. 4:23; cf. 9:35). By performing these kingdom miracles, Jesus was overthrowing Satan's kingdom. Every time he cast out a demon, healed a disease, or raised the dead, he was undoing the work of the devil. "If I drive out demons by the Spirit of God," Jesus said on one occasion, "then the kingdom of God has come upon you" (Matt. 12:28). In this way God's King began to restore God's rule over God's creation.

THE KING REJECTED

The more Jesus established God's kingdom, the more people started to treat him like a king. The crescendo of their praise built to a climax when Jesus rode into Jerusalem on a donkey. There the people gave him a royal welcome, spreading their garments in his path and shouting, "Blessed is the coming kingdom of our father David!" (Mark 11:10a). "Blessed is the king who comes in the name of the Lord!" (Luke 19:38a).

Before they could proceed to the coronation, however, Satan still had one or two tricks to play. For thousands of years he had tried to stop God's King from ever coming. In Bethlehem he tried to have him killed, but the King lived on. Out in the wilderness he tried to get him to abdicate, but the King stayed on his throne. There was nothing Satan could do to prevent his coming. Even when all else failed, there was still the chance Satan could persuade people to reject God's kingdom. Satan did this by persuading them to wish for the wrong kind of king. Although the people of Jerusalem were longing for God's kingdom to come, they did not understand what kind of kingdom it was. There were at least three things they failed to understand: the plan of the kingdom, the purpose of the kingdom, and the progress of the kingdom.

In the first place, people misunderstood God's *plan* for his kingdom, although the fact that Jesus was riding on a donkey should have given them a clue. They thought the kingdom would come the way kingdoms usually do: by the use of military force. But Jesus had a different strategy. It was a strategy not even Satan anticipated, although it was promised in the Scriptures: "See, your king comes to you, gentle" (Matt. 21:5; cf. Zech. 9:9). The kingdom of God would not come by power and might, but through suffering and death.

Second, people misunderstood the kingdom's *purpose*. They conceived of God's kingdom in political terms. They wanted Jesus to drive out the Romans. But God had a different purpose. He wanted to conquer the real enemies of humanity—sin, death, and the devil—and to establish his rule in the hearts of his people.

Third, people misunderstood the *progress* of the kingdom. They thought God's kingdom would come right away, which meant that their timing was off. They were right to wave their palms and shout "Hosanna!" The kingdom was coming. However, it would take more than a few days to get there. Sadly, most of them were not willing to wait that long. Before the week was out, they were calling for Jesus to be executed. Humanly speaking, it was people wishing for the wrong kind of kingdom that got Christ crucified.

I mention these misunderstandings because they have plagued the church from the time of Christ to this very day. Some Christians misunderstand God's *plan* for his kingdom. They want to establish it their own way rather than waiting for God to do it his way. God's way of establishing the kingdom is primarily through the preaching of the cross. But that does not seem very effective to most people. They would prefer to use force, which is the kind of thinking that leads to bloody crusades. Or they would rather entertain people into the kingdom, which is the kind of thinking that leads to man-centered worship.

Other Christians misunderstand the *purpose* of God's kingdom. They think of it in earthly terms, which usually means turning Christianity into some kind of political agenda. Whether that agenda happens to be liberal or conservative, the problem is not so much the agenda as it is the politics.

Since churches do not understand God's purpose for his kingdom, or his plan for achieving it, it is not surprising that they get frustrated with the *progress* of God's kingdom. They want the kingdom to hurry up and get here, and they become impatient when it seems so long in coming.

PRAYING FOR GOD'S KINGDOM

How can we come to a better understanding of God's kingdom? One of the best ways is by learning how to pray, "Your kingdom come." These three simple words from the Lord's Prayer explain the plan, the purpose, and the progress of God's kingdom.

This petition first helps us understand God's *plan* for ushering in his kingdom. The very fact that we are to *pray* for the kingdom proves that it is not the kind of thing we establish through our own efforts. It is something we must ask God to do because only he can do it.

God's plan was to establish his kingdom through his Son. Jesus Christ lived the perfect life we ought to have lived. He died the painful death we deserved to die. And when he had fully paid for all our sins, God raised him from the dead and exalted him to his kingly throne. Now that Christ is King, God does not tell us to go out and establish his kingdom, he invites us to enter it. This is why God's kingdom comes through the announcement that Christ, who was crucified, is now King. The kingdom comes mainly through proclamation.

The reason the church tries so many other things besides preaching Christ is because it suspects the kingdom can be established some other way. But there is no other way. People will not come into the kingdom because they like the minister, support the children's program, or enjoy the music. They may come into a church that way, but not into the kingdom. The only way people ever come into God's kingdom is by hearing his heralds proclaim a crucified King.

When you hear the glad news that Christ is King, the thing to do is to submit to his rule. When you repent for your sins and believe in Jesus Christ, God establishes his rule in your heart. This is part of what Jesus meant when he said, "the kingdom of God is within you" (Luke 17:21). Anyone who has ever entered that kingdom has done so by praying to God, "Your kingdom come" or words to that effect. That is the way the kingdom comes to you and the way you come into the kingdom. To become a Christian is simply to ask God to set up his throne as the supreme King of your heart. Spiros Zodhiates writes: "No other person, no power, no position, no possession should be allowed to rule in our heart. God must be the absolute and uncontested Sovereign. For it is imperative that His kingdom come in our hearts before it can come to rule in the world at large. Heaven must be in us before we can be in heaven. God's kingdom must be in us before we can be in God's kingdom. It must begin in our hearts."[3]

If you have not yet taken the step of inviting God to rule your heart, do not expect Satan to give you up without a fight. Until you come to Christ, you are a subject of Satan. As Martin Luther said, "we are wretched captives of powerful foes in strange lands. . . . All of us dwell in the devil's kingdom until the coming of the kingdom of God."[4] If you wish to come into God's kingdom, therefore, you must ask God to rescue you "from the dominion of darkness" and bring you "into the kingdom of the Son he loves" (Col. 1:13). You must renounce your deal with the devil and swear allegiance to Christ the King. You must say, in the beautiful words of hymnwriter Frances Havergal (1836–1879), "Take my heart, it is thine own; it shall be thy royal throne."

SEEKING GOD'S KINGDOM

The second petition of the Lord's Prayer also says something about the kingdom's *purpose*. We pray, "*Your* kingdom come." Thus we ask for *God's* kingdom to come, not our own.

A king has the right to rule his kingdom any way he likes, and God's kingdom is a kingdom of the heart. It is not a territory. It is not a party politic. It is not a nation-state with geographic borders. The kingdom of God is simply the rule of God. When we pray for God's kingdom to come, we are asking God to achieve his purpose of reigning as King in the hearts, minds, and wills of his loyal subjects.

Once we understand God's purpose for his kingdom, we can see that he wants to bring all of life under his sovereign rule. This is part of what it means to seek God's kingdom. As we have seen, we are first to pray for the kingdom. But we must do something more than pray for it, and that is to pursue it. Jesus said, "Seek ye first the kingdom of God" (Matt. 6:33, KJV).

It is through the common activities of daily life that God establishes his uncommon kingdom. God's kingdom may not be *of* this world (see John 18:36), but it is certainly meant to come *into* this world, and it does so in rather ordinary ways. Whenever you calculate the accounts payable, double-check a lab result, haul away the trash, serve a hot meal to the homeless, finish your history homework, help a customer find the right size, water the geraniums, or snap the lid on a sippy-cup, you are doing kingdom work. You are doing kingdom work provided, that is, you do whatever you do in submission to God's rule, for the sake of his royal honor. You are doing kingdom work, not because doing these things will necessarily change the world, but because by doing them, you show how God has changed you.

Seeking the kingdom also means praying for God to establish his rule around the world. It means asking God to use pastors, evangelists, missionaries, and church planters, and even you to spread the Gospel that transforms sinful rebels into his loyal subjects. The second petition of the Lord's Prayer is what gave the English Puritan Richard Baxter (1615–1691) his passion for missions. Praying for God's kingdom expanded Baxter's vision to encompass the entire world. He wrote: "I was wont to look but little beyond England in my prayers, as not considering the state of the rest of the world. . . . But now, as I better understand the case of the world and the method of the Lord's Prayer . . . I cannot be affected so much with the calamities of the land of my nativity as with the case of the heathen, Muslim and ignorant nations of the earth."[5] Anyone who comes under God's gracious rule wants to see everyone else come under it as well, until the kingdom of Christ covers the earth as the waters cover the sea.

THE KINGDOM TO COME

The last thing this petition helps us understand is the *progress* of God's kingdom. The petition "Your kingdom come" reminds us that the kingdom is not here yet, at least not in all its fullness. Otherwise, why would we still be praying for it to come?

In one sense, of course, the kingdom has already come because Jesus has come, and he is the King. But his rule has yet to achieve its widest extent. Therefore, writes Darrell Guder, "As we pray 'your kingdom come,' we affirm that Jesus Christ has triumphed over the powers of sin and death, but we also declare that the joy and freedom of life within the reign of God are not yet a full reality."[6] The kingdom of God, one might say, is a once and future kingdom. We are not praying for it to come into existence, but to come into dominance.

The progress of God's kingdom is gradual. It does not all come all at once, as Jesus was careful to explain to his disciples. In a number of his parables—like the mustard seed that gradually grows into a small tree, for example, or the yeast that slowly works all the way through the bread (Matt. 13:31-33)—the main point is the slow growth of the kingdom. We should not be discouraged, therefore, when we look around us and see how, in so many ways, the kingdom of God is not yet here. The troubles of the world simply send us back to our knees, back to the prayer Jesus taught us to pray. We are still praying for the kingdom of Christ to overcome the kingdom of this world.

The coming of the kingdom has often been compared to the way the Allies defeated Germany in 1944. For all intents and purposes, World War II was over on D-Day, when British and American troops established a beachhead in France. There were still battles to be fought, of course, and lives to be won and lost. But from that point on, the Germans were fighting a losing battle. All that remained was for the Allies to liberate Europe.

As far as the kingdom of God is concerned, D-Day was Good Friday. That was Satan's last mad attempt to defeat God's King and have him betrayed, tried, and nailed to the cross. But Satan was only able to wound him. By dying on the cross for our sins, Jesus actually struck a death-blow to sin, death, and the devil. Now the outcome of the battle between the two kingdoms is certain. All that remains is for God to liberate the captives of Satan's kingdom and bring them into the kingdom of his Son.

We live, therefore, "between the times." There is a temporal gap between the coming of God's kingdom and its climax. Theologians sometimes describe this delay as the "already" and the "not yet." God's kingdom has *already* come, but it is *not yet* here in all its glory. Christ has already come, but he has not yet come again. The Puritans described the same truth in a different way. They made a distinction between the "kingdom of grace" and the "kingdom of glory." These are not two different kingdoms, but one kingdom in two installments. In the words of Thomas Watson, "The kingdom of grace is nothing but the beginning of the kingdom of glory. The kingdom of grace is glory in the seed, and the kingdom of glory is grace in the flower."[7]

The kingdom of God's grace has already arrived. It was founded by the death and resurrection of Jesus Christ, and its gates are open wide to anyone who will call Christ the King. But we are still waiting for God's kingdom to come in all its glory, living in hope for the day when the kingdom of grace will become the kingdom of glory and Christ will be King over all. We long for the day Daniel prophesied, when "the sovereignty, power and greatness of the kingdoms under the whole heaven will be handed over to the saints, the people of the Most High. His kingdom will be an everlasting kingdom, and all rulers will worship and obey him" (Dan. 7:27).

Everything we have been saying about the coming of God's king-dom is perhaps best summarized in the *Westminster Shorter Catechism*, which reads: "In the second petition (which is, *Thy kingdom come*) we pray, That Satan's kingdom may be destroyed; and that the kingdom of grace may be advanced, ourselves and others brought into it, and kept in it; and that the kingdom of glory may be hastened" (A. 102). The word *hastened* is an appropriate word with which to end this chapter. We should not be surprised if the kingdom seems to come slowly. But it will come: make no mistake about that! Jesus even promised that it would come soon (Rev. 22:12). And as we wait for its coming, the prayer we often find on our lips is, "Come, Lord Jesus" (Rev. 22:20).

"Come, Lord Jesus" is the last prayer in the whole Bible. It is another way of praying the second petition of the Lord's Prayer: "Thy kingdom come." One day that prayer will be fully answered. Jesus Christ will come again as King to establish the "dominion that will not pass away and the kingdom that will never be destroyed" (Dan. 7:14b). He will gather all his loyal subjects around his throne, and he will say to them, "Come, you who are blessed by my Father; take your inheritance, the kingdom prepared for you since the creation of the world" (Matt. 25:34). Then the King will destroy the dominion of the devil, with all his unholy followers. The trumpets of angels will sound, and loud voices from heaven will say, "The kingdom of the world has become the kingdom of our Lord and of his Christ, and he will reign for ever and ever" (Rev. 11:15). Hallelujah! Amen.

For Discussion

1. What are some of the privileges and responsibilities of kings?

2. Give examples of how Jesus has those same rights and responsibilities in the kingdom of God. For example, Jesus has a throne (Isa. 66:1) and a crown (Rev. 14:14).

3. Jesus came into the world to establish God's kingdom. Read Matthew 18:3-4, 19:14, John 18:36, and Romans 14:17. From these passages, what can you tell about the nature of God's kingdom?

4. If you had been alive during Jesus' day, which aspects of God's kingdom that you mentioned in question 3 would have surprised you?

5. How were Jesus' miracles related to the kingdom of God? See Matthew 12:28 to guide your thinking.

6. Read Matthew 10:34-39. What is the purpose of God's kingdom?

7. In what specific ways are the purposes of God's kingdom being fulfilled today?

8. How is the purpose of God's kingdom misunderstood by some Christians today, and what effects does their misunderstanding have?

9. How does a fuller understanding of the plan and purpose of God's kingdom give you more patience with its apparently slow fulfillment?

10. What are some practical ways you can show that Christ is your king?

11. In Matthew 5:27-30 and 43-48, Jesus explains how the ethics of the kingdom of heaven differ from the law of Moses. Summarize what he says in your own words.

12. Without mentioning names, think of a person who is difficult to love. What are some practical ways you can show love to him or her?

13. If Jesus brought in the kingdom of God, why do we need to pray for God's kingdom to come?

14. Jesus told his disciples about the fulfillment of the kingdom of God in Matthew 24—25. What does Matthew 25:1-13 say about our responsibilities as we wait for the end times? What are some practical ways you can be ready for Christ's second coming?

15. The kingdom of God is most simply defined as the rule of God. With that in mind, what does it mean to pray for God's kingdom to come to the world?

16. What evidence is there of God's increasing rule over all aspects of your life? In what area(s) are you reluctant to give him control?

17. What are specific ways you can you pray this petition for your own life?

7

Your Will Be Done

*For I have come down from heaven not to do my will
but to do the will of him who sent me.*
JOHN 6:38

IMAGINE A WORK FORCE comprised entirely of angels. Not fallen angels, who hate God and his work, but perfect angels who always serve him with joyful praise. Angels on the payroll—it would be every employer's dream! For there are no slackers in heaven. Angels never go on strike. They never demand a raise or hold out for more benefits. They never call in sick, show up late, or take long coffee breaks. Angels never even complain. Night and day, they work as well as they can, as fast as they can, and as cheerfully as they can.

What makes angels such ideal employees is that they always follow their instructions. Consider the outstanding performance review they are given in Scripture:

> The LORD has established his throne in heaven,
>   and his kingdom rules over all.
> Praise the LORD, you his angels,
>   you mighty ones who do his bidding,
>   who obey his word.
> Praise the LORD, all his heavenly hosts,
>   you his servants who do his will.
>
> PSALM 103:19-21

Angels are God's best servants because they always do what he says. Whatever the command, they say, "Your will be done," and then they do it. By obeying God's every word, they make sure that his divine will is done in heaven.

DOWN TO EARTH

When we pray the way Jesus taught us to pray, we ask God to help us do his work on earth the way the angels do it in heaven: "Your will be done, on earth as it is in heaven" (Matt. 6:10). This is the third petition in the Lord's Prayer. It is the last of the "Thy" petitions: "Hallowed be *Thy* name, *Thy* kingdom come, *Thy* will be done" (KJV). Up to this point, the prayer has been all about God. We have prayed for God's name, God's kingdom, and God's will. From this point on we will pray for ourselves—our provision, our pardon, and our protection.

It is the third petition that brings the Lord's Prayer down to earth, making the transition from our Father up in heaven to his children down on earth. "In the third petition," explains the *Westminster Shorter Catechism*, "we pray, That God, by his grace, would make us able and willing to know, obey, and submit to his will in all things, as the angels do in heaven" (A. 103).

Be assured that God will answer this petition. Just as God's kingdom must come, so his will must be done. John Calvin said that among the first three petitions of the Lord's Prayer, "there is a great affinity and likeness. The hallowing of God's name is always attached to His reign, and the chief feature of His reign is to be acknowledged in the doing of His will."[1] Indeed, it is hard to see how God could grant one petition without granting the others. God's kingdom is God's rule, and how can God rule unless people obey his royal will? Wherever God's kingdom comes, there his will is done.

In one sense, of course, God's will is always done. How could it be otherwise? Since God is all-powerful, he does whatever he purposes to do. It is the very God-ness of God to do whatever he wants.

By his will God created the universe. "For you created all things," wrote the apostle John, "and by your will they were created" (Rev. 4:11). Having made this world, God does with it whatever he wills. The psalmist wrote, "The LORD does whatever pleases him, in the heavens and on the earth, in the seas and all their depths" (Ps. 135:6).

God does what he wills among the nations. Even the king of Babylon had to admit that "he does as he pleases with the powers of heaven and the peoples of the earth. No one can hold back his hand or say to him: 'What have you done?'" (Dan. 4:35b).

God does what he wills in redemption. From beginning to end, the whole plan of salvation unfolds according to the will of his eternal decree. It was God's will to choose a people in Christ before the foundation of the world. "In love he predestined us to be adopted as his sons through Jesus Christ, in accordance with his pleasure and will" (Eph. 1:5). It is God's will to justify sinners by faith, and then to sanctify them by his Word and Spirit (1 Thess. 4:3). Having willed to save his people, it is God's will to keep them safe to the very end. Jesus said, "And this is the will of him who sent me, that I shall lose none of all that he has given me, but raise them up at the last day. For my Father's will is that everyone who looks to the Son and believes in him shall have eternal life, and I will raise him up at the last day" (John 6:39-40).

On the last day, according to the will of God, every knee will bow, "in heaven and on earth and under the earth, and every tongue confess that Jesus Christ is Lord, to the glory of God the Father" (Phil. 2:10-11). It is God's will to receive universal praise. And when that day comes, the will of God will be done on earth as it is now done in heaven. His will *must* be done! The Bible teaches that God is the one "who works out everything in conformity with the purpose of his will" (Eph. 1:11). Therefore, our prayer for God's will to be done cannot go unanswered. Like all the other prayers of Scripture, it is based on the solid foundation of a divine promise.

MY WILL BE DONE?

In the meantime, God's will is not always done on earth. Otherwise, why would we need to pray for it? To understand why this is so, it helps to distinguish between God's *secret* will and God's *revealed* will. Theologians call God's *secret* will his "decree." God's decree is his eternal plan for everything he has created, a plan governed by the counsel of his secret will. God's *revealed* will is his command; it is God's law for our lives as it is set forth in the pages of Holy Scripture. The Bible is a revelation of the will of God. Ultimately, God will accomplish the secret will of his sovereign decree. But our problem, the problem that drives us to our knees, is that we live in a world where people do not obey the revealed will of God's command.

We ourselves are part of the problem. In our sinful nature, we do not want to obey the command of God's revealed will. In fact, we want the opposite. We do not seek after God, do not love him, and won't obey him. Whether we are with our family or our friends, whether we are at work or at rest, we want to have our own way rather than God's way.

This battle of the wills began when Adam first rebelled against God, and we joined the battle the moment we drew our first breath, if not before. From our father Adam we inherited a sinful nature, including a sinful will that is utterly opposed to the will of God. This is what Martin Luther and other theologians mean when they speak of "the bondage of the will." We cannot follow God's will because we are bound by the chains of selfish desire.

Wanting our own way has a negative influence on our prayers. Consider the mistake once made by the principal of one of the colleges in the University of Oxford. He was speaking at a meeting of the Oxford Inter-Collegiate Christian Union. While he was leading the students in the Lord's Prayer, he said: "Thy kingdom come, Thy will be done, on earth as it is in England." Or consider the mistake my brother-in-law made during a worship service. As he was singing the Lord's Prayer, he became aware that people had turned around to look at him in astonishment. Suddenly, he realized what had happened. He had just sung, as loudly and as joyfully as he could, "*My* kingdom come, *my* will be done!" Whether we realize it or not, that is often the way we come to God in prayer. Deep down, what we really want is for God to let us have our own way.

We need the third petition of the Lord's Prayer to show us how wrong it is to think of prayer as a way of getting something from God. People often think of prayer as a way of talking God into doing what they want him to do. This is what lies behind "name it and claim it" Christianity, the idea that I can influence God by offering the right kind of prayer. But that attitude ultimately leads to hell. As C. S. Lewis once observed, "There are only two kinds of people in the end: those who say to God, 'Thy will be done,' and those to whom God says, in the end, '*Thy* will be done.' All that are in Hell, choose it."[2] Besides, why would anyone want to change God's mind? The Bible says that his will is "good, pleasing and perfect" (Rom. 12:2). Imagine what a mess our lives would be in if God always did what we wanted him to do! For unlike God's will, our own wills are evil, displeasing, and imperfect.

It is much better for us to yield to the sovereign purpose of our loving heavenly Father who really does know best! Darrell Guder writes, "Prayer is not about getting what we want—the fulfillment of our will; it is about learning what God wants—the bending of our will to God's will."[3] The way we learn what God wants is by praying the third petition of the Lord's Prayer, in which we give up what our hearts desire to embrace his heart's desire.

THE ONE WHO CAME TO DO GOD'S WILL

Be forewarned that it is not always safe to pray the Lord's Prayer. When we pray, "Your will be done," we are yielding to God his right to do as he pleases. Often, that means praying for things we are not sure we want, or may not want at all. "Your will be done" is the kind of prayer that might lead to suffering, and even to death.

Consider what happened to the only man who ever totally surrendered to God's will: Jesus Christ. Jesus always did what God told him to do. His only purpose in life was to submit to the will of his Father in heaven. He came to do what we refused to do: Obey the will of God. Jesus said, "I have come to do your will, O God" (Heb. 10:7b). Indeed, the very reason he came down from heaven was to carry out the divine will: "I have come down from heaven not to do my will but to do the will of him who sent me" (John 6:38; cf. 5:30). And so he did. Jesus never sought his own glory. He always submitted to the Father's will for his life and ministry. He allowed himself to be led out into the wilderness to be tempted by the devil. He taught whatever God wanted him to teach. He performed whatever miracles God empowered him to perform. Doing God's will was like daily bread to him. "My food," said Jesus, "is to do the will of him who sent me and to finish his work" (John 4:34). For Jesus, doing God's will was life itself.

If you ever want to know what God's will is, just look at the life of God's Son. Cyprian, one of the early church fathers, wrote:

> Now that is the will of God which Christ both did and taught. Humility in conversation; steadfastness in faith; modesty in words; justice in deeds; mercifulness in works; discipline in morals; to be unable to do a wrong, and to be able to bear a wrong when done; to keep peace with the brethren; to love God with all one's heart; to love Him in that He is a Father; to fear Him in that He is God . . . this is to fulfil the will of the Father.[4]

Throughout his life Jesus always fulfilled the will of his Father. But his last and greatest surrender was death. The Bible teaches that Jesus "became obedient to death—even death on a cross" (Phil. 2:8). To understand the cost of that obedience, one has to go to the Garden of Gethsemane, where Jesus prayed the night before he was crucified. The prayers he offered in that garden were sheer agony. Jesus was in such great distress that he almost died that night—at least in his soul, if not in his body—for he said to his disciples, "My soul is overwhelmed with sorrow to the point of death" (Matt. 26:38).

In the garden Jesus wrestled with God's will for his life and his death. "My Father," he prayed, "if it is possible, may this cup be taken from me" (Matt. 26:39). Jesus knew what kind of cup it was, the cup of God's wrath against sin. If he went through with his crucifixion, he would have to drink it down to the bitter dregs, bearing the full weight of God's holy fury against sin. In doing so, Jesus would be separated from the fellowship he had enjoyed with his Father from all eternity. If ever a man wrestled with God's will, it was Jesus Christ, the God-man. Yet out of the depths of his woe, Jesus prayed the very prayer he teaches us to pray, not once, but twice. "Going a little farther, he fell with his face to the ground and prayed, 'My Father, if it is possible, may this cup be taken from me. Yet not as I will, but as you will'" (Matt. 26:39). "He went away a second time and prayed, 'My Father, if it is not possible for this cup to be taken away unless I drink it, may your will be done'" (Matt. 26:42).

Whenever we use this petition, we are offering a secondhand prayer. The reason we pray for the Father's will to be done is because Jesus prayed for it to be done. He first offered that prayer when he committed himself to die for our sins.

After he had said his prayers, Jesus allowed himself to be handed over to unjust men, men who had him betrayed, tried, convicted, mocked, beaten, and executed. Yet through these terrible events his prayers were answered. God's will *was* done. For it was the Father's will that the Son should suffer and die for our sins. This was promised through the prophet Isaiah, who wrote:

> It was the LORD'S will to crush him and cause him to suffer
>   and though the LORD makes his life a guilt offering,
> he will see his offspring and prolong his days,
>   and the will of the LORD will prosper in his hand.
>
> ISAIAH 53:10

God fulfilled the promise of Isaiah in the cross of Christ. The crucifixion was not a tragic mistake; it was God's plan for the salvation of sinners. When the apostle Peter preached to the very men who had Jesus executed, he said, "This man was handed over to you by God's set purpose and foreknowledge; and you, with the help of wicked men, put him to death by nailing him to the cross" (Acts 2:23). It was God's will that Jesus should be nailed to the cross and die for our sins. And because it was God's will, it was the answer to the prayer Jesus made for God's will to be done.

HAVE THINE OWN WAY, LORD

The way God answered Jesus' prayers in the Garden of Gethsemane was unique. It had to do with the once-and-for-all salvation of the world. But Jesus has given us permission to use his prayer, and just as his submission is the model for our surrender, so his petition is the pattern for our prayers.

In what specific ways is God calling you to pray for his will to be done? First, you must submit to God's will for your salvation. To pray, "Your will be done" is to admit that you need to be saved. For when we pray for God to do his will, we are admitting that we do not always do it. And if it is true that we do *not* do God's will, then we are sinners, and therefore in need of salvation. Martin Luther observed that when we pray the way Jesus taught us to pray,

> we judge and accuse ourselves with our own words, declaring that we are disobedient to God and do not do his will. For if we really did his will, this petition would not be necessary. It is really frightening to hear ourselves say, "Thy will be done." . . . If we pray in this manner, it is obviously true that we are not doing and have not done God's will. . . . So then, this petition brings about genuine humility and a fear of God and his judgment, and we are happy to escape God's judgment and to be saved by pure mercy and grace.[5]

God's mercy and saving grace are available to us through Jesus Christ alone. Submitting your will to God begins with putting your faith in Christ. It means believing that Jesus died on the cross for your sins and trusting that he was raised from the dead to give you eternal life.

Realize that when you put your faith in Jesus Christ, there can be no holding back. Your will must hand God its letter of resignation. For unless you submit to God's will in *everything*, you are not submitting to him in *anything*. Think about it. If you only follow God's will when it happens to correspond to your own will, then you never have to surrender at all. You are simply asking God to endorse your own agenda as often as he can. But if you want new life in Christ, you must adopt God's agenda and throw away your own.

Submitting to God's will for your salvation is only the beginning, however. When you pray, "Your will be done," you are committing yourself to God's will for every aspect of life and death. So in what other ways should you pray for God's will to be done?

Submitting to God's will means accepting the way God made you, with all your strengths . . . and all your weaknesses, and thus embracing who you are in Christ. God has a will for your *creation*. In his book *The Spiritual Life of Children*, Harvard sociologist Robert Coles describes meeting a little girl from Mississippi. The girl had just drawn her self-portrait in crayon. She pointed to it and explained, "That's me, and the Lord made me. When I grow up my momma says I may not like how He made me, but I must always remember that He did it, and it's His idea."[6]

The little girl's mother was teaching her daughter a valuable lesson about accepting God's will. If you were the Creator, you might have made "you" differently. But God has made you for his own pleasure. Every aspect of your personality, every feature of your appearance, every part of your body, every one of your talents and limitations has been given according to his exact specifications. The proper way to respond to the way God has made you is to say, "Lord, if this is who you made me to be, then your will be done."

Submitting to God's will means living by his Word. To put it another way, God has a will for your *sanctification*, your progress in personal holiness. By following his instructions, you show that you are one of his true sons or daughters. Jesus said, "Whoever does the will of my Father in heaven is my brother and sister" (Matt. 12:50). It is hard for us to do God's will the way Jesus did. So we must confess our unwillingness, as Jean-Pierre de Caussade (1675–1751) once did:

> Forgive me, divine Love, for . . . not having yet understood what it means to let your will be done. . . . I have been through all your galleries and admired all your paintings, but I have not yet surrendered myself sufficiently to be worthy to receive the strokes of your brush. . . . I will devote myself exclusively to the duty of the present moment to love you, to fulfil my obligations and to let your will be done.[7]

Like de Caussade, we must ask God to sanctify us by his Word, to "equip [us] with everything good for doing his will, and . . . work in us what is pleasing to him" (Heb. 13:21). When people ask how they can know God's will for their lives, I am sometimes tempted to hand them a Bible and say, "You want to know God's will for your life?

Here, start with this!" For it is as we keep God's law that he works in us "to will and to act according to his good purpose" (Phil. 2:13).

Submitting to God's will means going wherever he sends you, to do whatever he calls you to do. God has a will for your *vocation*. If you are one of his servants, then he has a job for you to do in his kingdom. A good example is Paul, whom God called to be an apostle to the Gentiles. Whenever Paul talked about his work, he mentioned that he was called to it "by the will of God" (e.g., 1 Cor. 1:1; Col. 1:1). He was an apostle because he had accepted God's will for his life. But one does not have to be an apostle to be called by God. God calls people to be investment bankers, jewelers, homemakers, forklift operators, sales clerks, lab technicians, and even preachers.

If you want to know what God wants *you* to do, the first question is not, "What is God's will for my life?" as if you have to read God's mind to know what you ought to do. Really, the first question about God's will is, "Am I willing to do it?" There is no sense asking for God to reveal his will for your life unless you are committed to doing what he wants done. This is where the Lord's Prayer helps us. Even though we do not know God's will for our future, we can still pray about it. The more we pray for God's will to be done, the more we yield ourselves to it.

THROUGH SUFFERING, INTO GLORY

Submitting to God's will means accepting whatever suffering God brings into your life. This, too, is part of his will. As it was for Christ, so it is for the Christian—God will not save you *from* suffering, but *through* suffering into glory.

A beautiful example of what it means to surrender to God in the midst of suffering comes from the life of John Newton (1725–1807). Every year on his birthday, Newton wrote a meditation describing what God was doing in his life. One year his thoughts were melancholy, for his wife was ill and he knew that she had not long to live. Newton could hardly bear to see his beloved suffer, but he resigned himself to God's will. At the end of his annual meditation, he wrote this simple prayer: "What thou wilt, when thou wilt, how thou wilt."[8]

In the end, submitting to God's will means accepting his purpose in death as well as in life. To pray for God's will to be done is to pray for God to glorify himself right to the very end of your life on this earth. One woman who submitted to God's will for her death was Jane Ewings. This godly woman was born and died in Surrey. We know very little else about her, except what we read on her tombstone:

> God made me and not myself; he created me for his pleasure, and at his pleasure he has disposed of me; he alone knows through what new scenes I must pass, and he will conduct me through them, so as to answer the end of his providence; I resign myself in full confidence on that Sovereign Being, who is just and merciful to all his creatures, and say not my will, but thine be done.

Another woman who surrendered her life and death to God's will was Betty Scott Stam, a missionary to China. Betty and her husband John were captured by the communists, stripped half-naked, and marched in chains through the streets of their village. Betty was forced to watch as her husband had his head chopped off. Then she herself was beheaded. Many years before her horrific martyrdom, Betty Scott Stam wrote the following prayer: "Lord, I give up all my own plans and purposes, all my own desires and hopes, and accept thy will for my life. I give myself, my life, my all utterly to thee, to be thine forever. Fill me and seal me with thy Holy Spirit. Use me as thou wilt. Send me where thou wilt, and work out thy whole will in my life at any cost, now and forever."[9]

In short, when we pray for God's will to be done, we are praying for his will to be done in *everything*. We are submitting to his will in all the circumstances of life and in death. This prayer is for our salvation, our vocation, and our sanctification. It is for our sufferings and our death.

We long for the day when we will be with God in his glory, when we will be unwilling to sin, when with all the saints and angels we will finally do God's will as it is done in heaven. The wonderful last verse of the hymn "Trust and Obey" expresses it like this: "Then in fellowship sweet, we will sit at his feet, or we'll walk by his side in the way; what he says we will do, where he sends we will go, never fear, only trust and obey." In the meantime, while we still live on earth and not in heaven, we pray for God to do with us what he wills, and to make of us what he chooses, in order to glorify himself as he pleases. What pleases God is nothing less than our total surrender.

Are you ready to submit your will to God? John Wesley (1703–1791) wrote a wonderful prayer of surrender to God's will. Wesley's yielding prayer has been used by many Methodist congregations at the first worship service of the new year. If you want God's will to be done in your life, then make this your prayer:

> I am no longer my own, but yours. Put me to what you will, rank me with whom you will; put me to doing, put me to suffering; let me be employed for you or laid aside for you, exalted for you or brought low for you; let me be full, let me be empty; let me have all things, let me have nothing; I freely and wholeheartedly yield all things to your pleasure and disposal.[10]

For Discussion

1. What do you think are the biggest problems facing our nation today?

2. How do God's instructions for life from the Bible specifically combat each of the societal problems that were mentioned, so that if his will were done, the problem would not exist? For example, if every person followed God's command to give to those in need, there would be no poverty.

3. How does praying for God's will to be done in specific situations change your attitude toward those circumstances?

4. Why do we need to pray for God's will to be done—isn't his will always done?

5. Read John 4:34. This verse reveals Jesus' heart attitude toward obedience. In what ways was God's will like food to him?

6. Share a time in your life when you, too, had a deep desire to obey God in a particular situation.

7. Jesus' obedience to God's will was tested in Matthew 26:36-46. Read that passage now. What words describe Jesus' emotional state during this story?

8. What was the "cup" that Jesus wanted God to take away?

9. What evidence do you see in this passage that Jesus' food was to do God's will? How is Jesus' deep desire to obey the Father's will evident in this narrative?

10. What enabled Jesus to desire God's will even in the midst of his anguish? Is there anything from his example of obedience that can help you to be more obedient?

11. How does this narrative enhance or change your understanding of the third petition of the Lord's Prayer?

12. In what areas is it hardest for you to submit to God by praying for his will to be done?

13. What step will you take this week toward greater submission to God?

8

Give Us Today Our Daily Bread

Give me neither poverty nor riches,
but give me only my daily bread.
PROVERBS 30:8b

PRAYING FOR DAILY BREAD may not seem very spiritual. The early church fathers were almost scandalized by the idea of making such a mundane request. Origen (c. 185–c. 254) thought daily bread was too "earthly and small" to pray about. He concluded it must therefore refer to the Word of God, which is the Bread of Life.[1] Jerome (c. 345–c. 419) called it "supersubstantial bread" rather than "daily bread." This meant that it was "more than physical," and therefore referred to the sacramental bread broken in the Lord's Supper.[2] For this reason, some early Christians celebrated daily Communion.

What the fathers could not quite bring themselves to see was how down-to-earth the fourth petition is. God cares for our physical needs as well as our spiritual needs. Body and soul—he redeems us, restores us, and raises us up again. Therefore, Jesus teaches us to pray for plain, old ordinary bread.

One theologian who did understand this was Tertullian, who noted "how gracefully has the Divine Wisdom arranged the order of the prayer; so that *after* things heavenly—that is, after the 'Name' of God, the 'Will' of God, and the 'Kingdom' of God—it should give earthly necessities also room for a petition!"[3] Jesus himself followed the same order only a few verses later, saying, "Seek first his kingdom and his righteousness, and all these things will be given to you as well" (Matt. 6:33). Once we have prayed for God's heavenly glory, then it is right for us to pray for our own earthly good.

GIVE . . .

"Give us this day our daily bread." This simple petition is profound in its teaching about God and its implications for the Christian life. Each word has something to teach. First, there is the word "give," which shows that even the most basic necessities of life are a gift from God.

Most of us have such an abundance of bread that we forget to pray for it. Some years ago now, a publisher wrote an essay to explain why he had given up on prayer. "I don't pray any more," he lamented. "I've given it up for Lent. Also for Advent and Pentecost. . . . How can I maintain, without lying, that God has a hand in this meal?"[4] Apparently, the man thought it would be somehow dishonest to pray for his daily bread. He had earned the paycheck. He had gone to the grocery store. He had untwisted the tie on the bread bag and made his sandwich. What did God have to do with it?

The truth is that everything we eat is a divine gift. Praying for God to give us our daily bread, then, is a matter of fundamental honesty. God is the one who waters the earth and causes the crops to grow. He is the one who gives us life and strength to earn our bread, and then to bake it. Thus our daily bread is not to be taken for granted. We are utterly dependent upon God's gracious provision every moment of every day.

We must work for our bread, of course. The Bible tells us that "If a man will not work, he shall not eat" (2 Thess. 3:10b). Toiling for our bread is part of God's curse against our sin, which forces us to eat our food by the sweat of our brow (Gen. 3:19a). But we can be redeemed from that curse by asking to receive our daily provision as a gift from God.

It is not only the poor who need to pray for their daily bread. Indeed, the more we have, the *more* we need this petition, not less. C. Stacey Woods wisely observes that "Material affluence in no respect lessens my need to rely on God. Actually, it increases it. I am in greater spiritual danger when I have plenty than when I have nothing. Hence the almost greater need of the wealthy to cry to God for mercy that they may not fail to trust him."[5] Saying grace before meals is a sign of spiritual maturity, for God's gift demands our gratitude.

. . . US . . .

The second important word in this fourth petition is the easiest to miss. "Give *us* this day our daily bread." There are times when we pray the Lord's Prayer in private. Just a few verses earlier, Jesus had told his disciples to go into their closets to pray (Matt. 6:6). But even when we pray in secret, the Lord's Prayer is never private.

Jesus taught his disciples to pray in the plural. He has given us a family prayer for the whole people of God. Therefore, when we pray for daily bread, we are not telling God, "Gimme, gimme, gimme." We are not praying for ourselves at all; we are praying for all Christians everywhere. The Dutch theologian Herman Witsius explained it like this: "As the word *our* is plural, it denotes a fellowship of love, by which every believer prays not only for himself, but for all the members of his family, for other believers who are his brethren, and for all men without exception, that they may enjoy the necessaries of life."[6] Praying for God to meet the needs of our brothers and sisters is part of what it means to believe in the communion of the saints.

It makes sense to pray for *our* bread because it takes a community to produce a loaf of bread. One person plows the field, plants the seed, and harvests the grain. Another person grinds the flour and bakes the bread. Still others deliver the loaf to the dinner table. Thus most of the bread we eat, at least in America, was made by someone else. "Every time we ask God for bread, we are acknowledging not only our dependence upon a beneficent God but also our dependence on other people. No bread comes to our table without the work, the sacrifice, and the gifts of strangers whom we do not know, and cannot thank."[7]

By asking God to give "us" our bread, we also identify with the poor, especially the Christian poor. In this culture of consumption we often forget the hungry. But we live in a needy world. There are places in Asia, Africa, the Middle East, and South America where our own brothers and sisters are starving. Food for the world is a matter for prayer. Hunger is not an agricultural problem, by and large, but a spiritual problem. There is more than enough food to feed the world. Yet people still go hungry. The poor lack bread because of greed, sloth, corruption, oppression, and warfare. That is why the church prays for bread. First we pray for God's kingdom to come and make things right. Then wherever God's kingdom comes our prayers are answered, not only for the kingdom, but also for bread.

When we pray for God to give us bread, we are also committing ourselves to share it when we get it. Otherwise, our prayer is insincere. How can we pray, "Give us this day our daily bread," and then refuse to provide what the rest of "us" need? If I am to pray this prayer honestly, I must be willing to become part of its answer. This is what the apostle James was talking about when he said, "Suppose a brother or sister is without clothes and daily food. If one of you says to him, 'Go, I wish you well; keep warm and well fed,' but does nothing about his physical needs, what good is it?" (James 2:15-16). Getting daily bread for yourself may seem like a physical matter, but giving daily bread to others is a spiritual matter.

It was Basil the Great (c. 329–379) who said, "The bread that is spoiling in your house belongs to the hungry. The shoes that are mildewing under your bed belong to those who have none. The clothes stored away in your trunk belong to those who are naked."[8] Therefore, I must feed the hungry. I must show hospitality to the homeless. I must send some of my bread to my brothers and sisters who have nothing to eat.

. . . TODAY . . .

The bread we ask God to give us all is bread for today. Here we come to the most difficult word in the entire prayer. The word is the Greek term *epiousion*, and the only place it appears in the entire New Testament is here in the Lord's Prayer (Matt. 6:11; Luke 11:3). In fact, this is the only place where the word appears in all of Greek literature, which explains why Origen figured the disciples must have made it up.[9]

For the last two thousand years, Bible scholars have struggled to know exactly what *epiousion* means. One possibility is that it means something like "essential," or "sufficient." In other words, it refers to whatever bread is necessary for daily life. We are asking God to give us what we need: "Give us today the bread necessary for our existence."[10]

Another possibility is that *epiousion* means "immediately following." In other words, it might refer to the following day. Thus Donald Carson translates the verse like this: "Give us today our bread for the coming day."[11] This translation made good sense in the ancient world, where prayers were offered in the evening as well as the morning. This petition would work for both. "Give us today our bread for the coming day." In the morning we pray for what we need for the dawning day; in the evening we pray for God's provision on the morrow.

Ernst Lohmeyer concludes that the fourth petition is the prayer of "a poor man who in the morning does not know how he will nourish himself and his family beyond the day, or of a traveller who begins his journey early without bread or money or purse, or even of a day-labourer who waits in vain for work in the market place."[12] The idea of the coming day fits well with what we know about ancient cuisine. There were no "use by" dates in the time of Christ. It was "the Near Eastern custom, at least in simple circles, to bake each day only the necessary unleavened bread for the day, so that what is baked in the morning is consumed by the evening; it does not calculate on keeping food for a meal which goes beyond today."[13]

All things considered, the best translation is probably the one William Tyndale gave in 1525, and which English Bibles have used ever since: "daily bread." We are asking God to give us bread for the coming day. Whether this means today's bread or tomorrow's bread, it is still daily bread. This translation has since been confirmed by ancient Egyptian manuscripts. In 1925 archaeologists discovered a papyrus with the word *epiousion*. It was an account of daily rations, almost like a grocery list. More recently, scholars have found a papyrus from someone who ran errands to Alexandria to get some provisions, including *epiousion* and "other things pertaining to everyday life."[14]

There is still one more reason for stating that "daily bread" is the best translation. This petition from the Lord's Prayer echoes a prayer from the Old Testament, a saying of Agur from the book of Proverbs: "Give me neither poverty nor riches, but give me only my daily bread" (Prov. 30:8b). When we pray the Lord's Prayer, we are asking God to give us what we need for today.

One of the things we discover as we read the Bible is that God's people often had to live one day at a time. After God led his people out of Egypt, he gave them bread from heaven, the manna in the wilderness (Exod. 16). The amazing thing about manna was that it could only be eaten that day. If it was kept overnight, it would spoil. Or consider the way God provided for Elijah by the brook (1 Kings 17). When that great prophet went to live in the Kerith Ravine, ravens brought him bread and meat twice a day. Then Elijah went to Zarephath to live with a hungry widow who was down to her last meal. But God put flour in her jar and oil in her jug, "so there was food *every day* for Elijah and for the woman and her family" (1 Kings 17:15). What these two miracles have in common is not just bread, but daily bread. They show that there are times when God's people have to live from hand-to-mouth, the way the first Christians lived in Jerusalem. These early believers were so poor that the apostles organized a daily distribution of food (Acts 6:1). By living day-to-day, they learned to trust God constantly for everything.

Have you learned the same lesson? Do you live in daily dependence on God's provision? The Bible has a word for someone who demands more than what he needs for today. The word is "fool." Jesus told a story about just such a man:

> The ground of a certain rich man produced a good crop. He thought to himself, "What shall I do? I have no place to store my crops." Then he said, "This is what I'll do. I will tear down my barns and build bigger ones, and there I will store all my grain and my goods. And I'll say to myself, 'You have plenty of good things laid up for many years. Take life easy; eat, drink and be merry.'" But God said to him, "You fool! This very night your life will be demanded from you. Then who will get what you have prepared for yourself?"
>
> LUKE 12:16-20

The man was a fool because he craved something more than his daily bread. He did not recognize the basic poverty of his existence, that he needed God every moment of every day for everything he had.

This does not mean that Christians always have to live at the subsistence level, or that we may not plan for the future. When Elisha helped a widow, for example, God gave her jars and jars full of oil so she could live off the proceeds indefinitely (2 Kings 4:1-7). The Bible also commands us to plan for our children's future, if we are able (Prov. 13:22).

What this petition does mean, however, is that we should not worry about the future. As Jesus later commanded, "Do not worry about tomorrow, for tomorrow will worry about itself" (Matt. 6:34). In his grace, God often gives us much more than we need, but sometimes his care for us will be "day of." As far as our lives on this earth are concerned, all he has promised is daily bread. We should pray, therefore, the way the Dutch theologian Hugo Grotius (1583–1645) prayed: "Give us, O God, the food that is necessary for the remainder of life. If it please thee not to give us yearly, give us monthly, give us at least daily supplies. Every thing beyond this will be superfluous."[15] If God wants to give us any more than we need, that is his business.

. . . OUR DAILY BREAD

This brings us to the final word in this petition: bread. Actually, in the Greek original, the word "bread" comes first, for bread is what the petition is all about. A literal translation might go like this: "Our bread for the coming day, give us today."

We are to pray for bread. Bread is food at its most basic level. Whether it comes in a roll, a loaf, a cracker, a bagel, a crumpet, a rice cake, or a tortilla, every culture in the world makes some kind of bread. It is one of the staples of life. When we ask God for bread, therefore, we are not asking for an extravagance. According to the *Westminster Shorter Catechism*, "In the fourth petition (which is, *Give us this day our daily bread*) we pray, That of God's free gift we may receive a competent portion of the good things of this life, and enjoy his blessing with them" (A. 104). We do not ask God for too much or too little, but "a competent portion."

The Bible uses the term *bread* to describe whatever food we really and truly need to live. Jesus teaches us to ask for bread, not dessert. Gregory of Nyssa (330–c. 395) explained it like this: "We are commanded to seek what is necessary for the preservation of the bodily existence, by saying to God, *Give bread*, not luxury, nor wealth, nor beautiful purple robes, nor ornaments of gold,—nor anything else by which the soul might be drawn away from its divine and worthier care, but—*bread*."[16]

Our trouble is that so often we come to God with our greeds rather than our needs. Already having everything we need, we pray for what we want. This becomes the source of our discontent: we desire things that God has not promised.

The fourth petition of the Lord's Prayer brings us back down to earth. As we pray, Jesus teaches us that bread is enough for us. As the Scripture says, "If we have food and clothing, we will be content with that" (1 Tim. 6:8). Even if all we have is a little food to make it through the day, we still have all we need.

Because bread is something we really do need, God will certainly give it to us. The reason Jesus taught us this petition was because he *knew* that God would answer it. He is the God who "gives food to the hungry" (Ps. 146:7), who has promised to "meet all your needs according to his glorious riches in Christ Jesus" (Phil. 4:19).

Have you ever gone without daily bread? Not, I expect, if you have prayed for it. I think, for example, of a single mother from our church who went out with her little girl to get some food. She was hoping to get a sandwich and a drink, maybe some chips. She went first to the cash machine, where she discovered that there was a problem with her accounts. She had no money for bread. As she walked slowly and sadly away, she said "I'm sorry, baby, we don't have any money."

This was hard for a five-year old to accept, so the girl started to protest. Her mother threw up her hands and said, "What do you want me to do? I don't have any money!"

The little girl said just one word: "Pray." So her mother looked up into the blue sky and prayed that somehow God would make a way, that he would give them ten dollars for a meal. After she prayed she decided to go back to the cash machine to get a printout of her account, which she did, but still there was no money, so they started to go home.

As they were walking down the street, a woman came up from behind. She could tell they were having some kind of trouble, so she asked what was wrong. When the woman heard they had no money, she reached into her purse and said, "Will you take a loan?" While the mother was figuring out how to pay her back, the woman said, "Only don't think of it as a loan—think of it as God telling me to give it to you."

It is the Father's pleasure to take care of the needs of his children. Remember that you are praying to your Father in heaven, who loves you in Jesus Christ. The petition for daily bread thus implies a promise, the promise that the Father will provide whatever his children actually need.

The great missionary to China, Hudson Taylor, learned about God's fatherly care from his own experience as a father. He wrote in one of his journals:

> I am taking my children with me, and I notice that it is not difficult for me to remember that the little ones need breakfast in the morning, dinner at midday, and something before they go to bed at night. Indeed I *could* not forget it. And I find it *impossible* to suppose that our heavenly Father is less tender or mindful than I. . . . I do not believe that our heavenly Father will ever forget His children. I am a very poor father, but it is not my habit to forget my children. God is a very, very good Father. It is not His habit to forget His children.[17]

The promise of God's fatherly provision is not just for bread, it is for all our everyday needs. "Bread" includes everything that is necessary for the body. It certainly includes clothing, and perhaps shelter. It covers health and gainful employment, the strength and work we need to earn our bread. Whatever we truly need, God will supply.

The great Bible teacher Harry Ironside (1876–1951) told a wonderful story about the way God meets all our needs.[18] It concerned a pious old Scotsman traveling to worship in Aberdeen. Along the way the old man met a young seminary student. When the two men sat down for lunch, the old man suggested that they each pray to ask God for what they needed. The young man was somewhat embarrassed by this suggestion, but he allowed his elder to pray.

The old man had three requests. First, as he was hard of hearing, he asked God for a seat near the front of the church when they arrived. Second, he reminded the Lord that he was badly in need of new shoes, yet was unable to pay for them. Finally, he asked for a bed to sleep in that night. The old man not only prayed for these things, but thanked God in advance for providing them. The seminary student was so appalled by the impertinence of making such specific requests that he determined to find out what became of the old man's prayers.

The men arrived late to the meeting, and there was not a seat to be found. The old man stood at the back of the church with his hand cupped to his ear, straining to listen, while the student thought to himself, "We will see now what becomes of such prayers!"

Just then a young lady in the front row happened to notice the old man and called for an usher. "Sir," she said, "my father asked me to save this seat for him, saying that if he should be late I should offer it to someone else. Evidently he has been detained. Will you please go and offer it to that old man who has his hand to his ear and is standing just inside the door." Within moments, the old man's first request was granted.

Before long it came time to pray. When the old man knelt to say his prayers, the young woman noticed that his shoes were worn completely through. Now the woman's father happened to be a cobbler. So immediately after the service she asked the man if she could take him to her father's shop and give him a pair of shoes, which she proceeded to do. While they were standing in the shoe shop, the young woman inquired where the old man was spending the night. He answered that God had not yet shown him the room. "Well," she said, "I think we have the room for you. The Rev. Dr. So-and-So was to use our guest room tonight, but he has telegraphed to say that he is not coming. Will you use it?"

The next day, when the seminary student inquired how the old man had made out, he learned that all three of his prayers had been answered. He also learned that when God's children pray for daily bread, God grants them the simple necessities of life.

THE BREAD OF LIFE

We began this chapter by emphasizing that daily bread is simply that: daily bread. It is important not to over-spiritualize this prayer by thinking that it refers primarily to the Word of God or to the bread of Communion. The bread we eat every day is a gift from God, a sign of his loving care for all his children. Yet for the Christian, bread can never be merely bread. Bread is a matter of life and death. We must eat to live. Therefore, the gift of our daily bread teaches us to depend on God for life itself, not only physically, but also spiritually.

Jesus tried to teach people this lesson after he fed the 5,000. They were so impressed with his miracle that they wanted to sign up for a permanent meal plan. "Sir," they said, "from now on give us this bread" (John 6:34).

Jesus answered, "I *am* the bread." He was saying something like this: "You have to understand, there is more to life than daily bread. What you really need is life itself, not just now, but forever, and I am the only one who can give it to you."

However real daily bread seems to us, it is still not the reality; it is only the picture. Jesus Christ is the reality. Jesus said to them, "I tell you the truth, unless you eat the flesh of the Son of Man and drink his blood, you have no life in you. Whoever eats my flesh and drinks my blood has eternal life, and I will raise him up at the last day. For my flesh is real food and my blood is real drink" (John 6:53-55). Jesus was speaking spiritually, of course. He was saying that what he did on the cross—offering his own body and blood for our sins—is the food and drink of eternal life. Anyone who wants to live forever with God must take Jesus in the way a hungry man takes in his daily bread.

We may never fully understand what is meant by the bread of life, but we can experience it by eating the Lord's Supper. When we receive Communion, the bread on the table is physical bread, but it also has a spiritual meaning. The bread is an aftertaste of salvation. It reminds us of the body that was given for our sins on the cross. It is also a fore-taste of the kingdom to come, when we will sit down with Jesus at his eternal banquet and eat the bread of heaven.

Jesus took the bread and said, "This is my body" (Matt. 26:26) because he is the real bread. What joy there is to life when we discover that he is all we need, and that having him, there is nothing we lack. Jesus declared, "I am the bread of life. He who comes to me will never go hungry" (John 6:35a).

For Discussion

1. Having prayed for heavenly things—the name of God, the will of God, and the kingdom of God—Jesus turns to the earthly necessity of bread. Have you ever wondered whether or not your basic necessities would be met for a given day? Describe the circumstances. If you have never been in that situation, tell about the time you were most thankful for a meal and why.

2. Make a list of the things you pray for most regularly.

3. Looking at the list you just made, in what areas of life are you most aware of your dependence on God?

4. This prayer starts out with the word "give," which shows that even the most basic necessities of life are gifts from God. What are some ways to remind yourself that everything you have is ultimately a gift from God?

5. Read James 2:15-16. What important truth does the word "us" in this petition show?

6. One man who understood the meaning of "daily bread" was Elijah. Read his story in 1 Kings 17:1-16. What methods did God use to provide Elijah with "daily bread"? What do those methods teach us about God and how he provides for us?

7. Why do you think God chose to provide for Elijah on a day-by-day

basis rather than in a more abundant way? What lessons does daily provision teach us that we wouldn't learn if our needs were always cared for in advance?

8. What do the reactions of Elijah and the widow tell you about their character?

9. In what ways has God provided for you on a day-by-day basis? Share your story.

10. What spiritual lessons does God teach through making people rely on him for daily needs?

11. Jesus told a story about a man who thought he didn't need God to provide for his daily needs. Read about it in Luke 12:15-21. What words describe this man?

12. What was this man's sin?

13. Looking especially at verses 15 and 21, what is the point of this parable?

14. Based on this parable and the passage on worry that immediately follows it in verses 22-34, what do you think our attitude toward wealth and financial planning should be?

15. Why did Jesus choose to use the word "bread" in the Lord's Prayer—what does it include?

16. Do you find it easy to trust God to provide for your needs? Why or why not?

17. Is there anything in your life that would suggest a sinful attitude toward wealth? Confess this to God.

9

Forgive Us Our Debts

*If we confess our sins, he is faithful and just
and will forgive us our sins.*
1 JOHN 1:9a

ONE OF THE FIRST TIMES I worshiped in a church from another Christian denomination than mine, what surprised me most was the wording of the fifth petition of the Lord's Prayer: "Forgive us our trespasses, as we forgive those who trespass against us." This surprised me because I had been raised Presbyterian, and good Presbyterians ask God to forgive their "debts," not their "trespasses."

Both terms obviously have something to do with sin, which is the word Luke uses in his version of the Lord's Prayer: "Forgive us our sins, for we also forgive everyone who sins against us" (Luke 11:4a). But the word "trespass," even though it may sound more elegant than the word "debt," is biblically inaccurate and theologically incomplete. It is biblically inaccurate because the word used in Matthew's version of the Lord's Prayer is in fact the Greek word for "debt" (*opheilhma*) and not "trespass" (*paraptoma*). (As we shall see in the next chapter, the word "trespass" does show up in the explanation that follows the Lord's Prayer in Matthew 6:14-15). This is why most English versions, including the King James, translate the Lord's Prayer like this: "Forgive us our debts" (Matt. 6:12a).

"Trespass" is also theologically incomplete. It suggests that sin is simply a matter of going too far, of stepping over the line or infringing on God's property rights. That is true, as far as it goes. To sin *is* to transgress; it is to overstep the boundaries of God's law.

However, trespassers can sometimes manage to get off private property before they get into trouble. That is not the case with those who sin against Almighty God. Once we sin, we remain in God's debt, even after we are finished committing the sin. We are not just trespassers, we are debtors.

IN GOD'S DEBT

The best thing to do when you fall into debt is to see a financial counselor. The first thing the counselor will do is calculate the full extent of your indebtedness. You have to know how much you owe before you can begin paying it. Since we find ourselves in God's debt, we need to know exactly how much we owe him.

There is a sense in which we owe everything to God. We owe him our existence. Our very lives are on loan from him, for he is the one who made us and sustains us. We are indebted to God for our gifts and talents, for our daily bread, and for every other good thing. Thomas Kelly (1769–1854) wrote,

> Praise the Savior, ye who know him!
> Who can tell how much we owe him?
> Gladly let us render to him all we are and have.

We owe God our thanks and praise for everything he has given us (which is, after all . . . everything).

Since we are God's creatures, we also owe him our perfect obedience. We must give God his due. The mere fact that he made us gives him the right to demand our allegiance. "Why ought you to glorify God?" asks the fifth question in the *Children's Catechism*. The answer is, "Because he made me and takes care of me." The God who brought you into existence deserves your wholehearted obedience.

The trouble with us, however, is that we do not glorify God and will not obey him. Our loyalties are divided. We would rather love ourselves than serve God. In a word, we are sinners, and our guilt places us still further into God's debt.

Consider how many debts we have accrued through our sin.

There is, first of all, the debt of *original sin*. Original sin is the term theologians use to describe the sinful nature we have inherited from our father Adam. The Bible teaches that "through the disobedience of the one man the many were made sinners" (Rom. 5:19a). This verse shows the unbreakable connection between Adam's sin and our sin. It means that the guilt of Adam's first sin has been imputed to us, or charged to our account. Even if we never committed any sins of our own, we would still be liable for the sin of Adam. But we *have* committed sins of our own. The debt of original sin is compounded by the debt of *actual sins,* which perhaps explains why the word "sins" occurs in the plural in this petition: "Forgive us our *sins.*" We are sinners in our own right, adding our own personal guilt to the guilt we inherited from Adam.

We are guilty both for what we have done and for what we have left undone, for sins of omission as well as commission. Our debt includes secret sins as well as public ones, deliberate sins as well as sins committed in ignorance. We have not kept what Jesus called the two greatest commandments: love for God and love for neighbor (Matt. 22:37-39). We have not loved God with all our heart, soul, mind, and strength. Nor have we loved our neighbors as ourselves, if we have loved them at all.

The two greatest commandments, in turn, can be subdivided into the Ten Commandments—four for the love of God and six for the love of neighbor. We have broken these as well. We have put other deities in God's place. We have cursed our Creator and the world he has made. We have been angry with people, even hated them. We have indulged in various kinds of sexual sin. We have taken things that did not belong to us. We have stretched the truth. In short, we have sinned in every way, shape, and form, and every sin adds to the sum total of our indebtedness. When the Dutch theologian Herman Witsius considered the extent of our moral bankruptcy, he sadly wrote, "We are chargeable with *debts,*—debts of every description,—Original, imputed, inherent;—actual,—debts of omission and commission, of ignorance, infirmity, and deliberate wickedness, without limits and without number."[1]

To make a thorough accounting, however, we would have to add all the sins we commit in cooperation with others. The Lord's Prayer is not an act of private devotion. It is a corporate prayer, intended for the public use of God's people. Notice that there are four plural pronouns in this one brief petition: "Forgive *us our* debts, as *we* also have forgiven *our* debtors." Our prayer for God's forgiveness is intended to be offered in unison.

We need to add, therefore, all the sins of the historical church. We have been guilty of factions and divisions. We have embarked on unjust crusades and defended unworthy causes. We have been careless in our theology and loveless in our practice. We have been timid in our witness, so that after 2,000 years our one Great Commission—the evangelization of the world—still remains unfinished.

Then think of all the sins the church continues to commit every single day. All the devotions left unread and petitions left unprayed. All the songs and hymns sung in half-hearted praise. All the proud thoughts. All the unkind remarks. All the poor people passed by in the road. All the evangelistic opportunities squandered through lack of courage.

When all our sins are added together, they place us in God's eternal debt. For we are obligated to keep God's law, and whenever we break that law, we become liable to its penalty—the wrath and curse of God. Witsius explained it like this: "Man's first debt is obedience to God. When that debt has not been paid, it is followed by another debt of sin, by which the sinner owes a debt to Divine justice."[2] When we pray the way Jesus taught us to pray, therefore, we come as guilty sinners. We accept our legal status as God's debtors. We agree that we deserve to receive just punishment for our sins.

Since we are in such great debt, perhaps we may think of the final judgment as a bankruptcy trial. In former times, at the beginning of a bankruptcy proceeding, it was customary for the bailiff to walk into the courtroom and say, "All debtors rise!" Imagine every man, woman, or child who ever lived gathering before the throne of God's justice. Imagine our great Judge taking his seat, while an angel says, "All debtors rise!" At those words, every human being would have to stand before the Judge to settle his debts for all eternity.

MORE THAN WE CAN PAY

The first thing to do with an enormous debt is to figure out exactly how enormous it is. The next thing is to set up a plan to begin paying it off. As any financial counselor will tell you, even if you can't get rid of your debts all at once, it is imperative to start making payments as soon as you can.

As soon as we start trying to figure out how to pay God what we owe for our sins, we realize how much trouble we are really in. Obviously, we cannot pay off our debts by ourselves. How could we ever make up for all the sins we have committed? Yet this is precisely the error most religions make, including false versions of Christianity. They all operate on the basis that human beings can do something to make things right with God. Their reasoning goes something like this: "Lord, I know I keep messing up, but I'm trying really, really hard to be good. In case you haven't noticed, I have a list here of some of the good things I've done—charitable work, and that sort of thing. Yes, I know my list isn't as long as it could be, but why don't we just call it even?" This kind of approach to God is based on the principle of works righteousness, the idea that doing good works can make someone good enough for God.

The truth is, however, that forgiveness is not something we can work for, it is only something we can ask for. Even if we worked for all eternity, laboring in the very pit of hell, we could never work off the debt we owe to God. What could we ever pay to God? Jesus posed the question this way: "What can a man give in exchange for his soul?" (Matt. 16:26b). The answer, of course, is nothing. Our souls are the most valuable thing we have. When, because of our sin and guilt, we owe God our very souls, there is nothing left for us to pay.

No one else can pay for us, either. Everyone else has his own debts to worry about. The whole world is full of God's debtors. We see them all around us, running up their charges with their selfish ambition at work, their angry words at home, and their petty disputes in the church. The more people sin, the more debt they accumulate. Thus, when it comes to your spiritual accounts, no one can help you because no one else has any more assets than you do! The psalmist wrote,

No man can redeem the life of another
or give to God a ransom for him—
the ransom for a life is costly,
no payment is ever enough.

PSALM 49:7-8

Asking someone else to settle your account with God would be like asking for financial help from a man heading for bankruptcy court.

DEAR DAD, SEND MONEY

This is our financial condition, spiritually speaking: We owe God far more than we or anyone else could ever pay. So where can we turn for help?

Sometimes, when people get into real financial difficulty, they ask their parents for help. I think of the penniless young man who sent a letter to his father from college. He thought about simply writing, "Dear Dad, Send money!" but decided that would be too obvious. Instead, he wrote a rather ordinary letter home, but whenever he came to the letter "S," he used the dollar sign ($) on his typewriter. His father got the point and sent a check right away. The Lord's Prayer works the same way. From beginning to end, the whole prayer is addressed to our Father in heaven. When we ask for our debts to be forgiven, therefore, we are asking our *Father* to forgive them.

Jesus once told a story about a young man who fell into debt. We mentioned this story back in chapter 4, but thinking of it in terms of indebtedness yields several new insights. As you may recall, the young man was sick of home, tired of living under the authority of his father. He decided to ask for his share of the inheritance before the old man died. Even to make such a request was a complete disgrace to the family. So it was with a broken heart that the father counted out his son's share of the estate. The young man took the money and ran away from home. When he got to a far country he wasted his wealth on wild living. He was just plain sick, suffering from the ill effects of his sinful nature. Soon the entire inheritance was spent and he fell into bankruptcy.

In desperation, the young man went out and did what his father probably had always wanted him to do: he started looking for a job. He was able to find a temporary position working on a pig farm. It was a miserable business, but he had no choice. He was so hungry that there were even times when he craved a couple bites of hog chow. Then one day, as he was slopping the pigs, he suddenly realized that he was homesick. Not sick of home, as he had once been, but actually homesick. The young man's thoughts went back to his father. Jesus told the story like this: "When he came to his senses, he said, 'How many of my father's hired men have food to spare, and here I am starving to death! I will set out and go back to my father and say to him: Father, I have sinned against heaven and against you. I am no longer worthy to be called your son; make me like one of your hired men'" (Luke 15:17-19).

So the young man set off for home, hoping his dad would give him a job in the family business. There was only one flaw in his thinking: he underestimated his father's capacity for forgiveness. True, the speech he was rehearsing to give when he arrived back home was a confession of sin, more or less. But the young man was still thinking like a debtor, expecting to have to work off his debts. He assumed the best he could hope for was to become one of his father's farmhands. Then the son caught sight of the family farm, off in the distance. Strange to say, there was a man running towards him, a man with his robes hitched up in the most undignified manner. Why, it was his father! "While he was still a long way off, his father saw him and was filled with compassion for him; he ran to his son, threw his arms around him and kissed him" (Luke 15:20b).

Once his dad was finished kissing him, the son made his little speech: "Father, I have sinned against heaven and against you. I am no longer worthy to be called your son" (Luke 15:21). But there was no talk then of becoming a hired hand. It was all robes and sandals, golden rings and fatted calves. There was no need for the son to slave away in his father's fields; he had been welcomed into the embrace of his father's forgiveness. For this is what forgiveness means: "To let go without a sense of guilt, obligation, or punishment."[3]

This is precisely what we ask God to do in the fifth petition of the Lord's Prayer. We ask our Father to forgive us our debts. With these words we declare our moral bankruptcy, freely admitting that we owe God more than everything we have. Then we do the only thing we can, which is ask him to forgive us outright. Because he is our loving Father, God does what we ask. "He does not treat us as our sins deserve or repay us according to our iniquities. . . . As a father has compassion on his children, so the LORD has compassion on those who fear him" (Ps. 103:10, 13). God the Father offers forgiveness as a free gift of his grace. When you go to him, weighed down with the debt of all your guilt and sin, he will not sit down with you to work out a payment plan. He will not scheme to charge you more interest. He will not send you to Purgatory or anywhere else to work off your debts. On the contrary, God is a loving Father who offers forgiveness full and free.

NAILED TO THE CROSS

Understand that when God remits our debts, he is well within his legal rights. The Scripture says that "if we confess our sins, he is faithful and just and will forgive us our sins" (1 John 1:9a). The reason God can justly forgive is because his children's debts have already been paid.

This is why Jesus Christ came into the world. God the Father grants forgiveness through God the Son. This is the meaning of the triumphant words in Paul's letter to the Colossians: "God made you alive with Christ. He forgave us all our sins, having canceled the written code, with its regulations, that was against us and that stood opposed to us; he took it away, nailing it to the cross" (Col. 2:13b-14).

These verses explain precisely how God forgave our debts. They speak of a "written code." In the Roman world, the Greek word for "written code" (*cheirographon*) referred to any handwritten signature. But it had a specialized meaning in the world of finance. There it referred to a certificate of debt signed in the debtor's own hand, what today we would call an "I.O.U." A man would write out how much money he owed, and then he would attach his signature to it.

When the apostle Paul spoke of this certificate of debt, he called it "the written code, with its regulations." Obviously, what he meant by the "written code" was the law of God, with all its regulations for human conduct. What God's law tells us is how much we owe to God. The two great commandments that sum up the law require us to love God and our neighbor. The Ten Commandments obligate us to worship God, honor our parents, preserve the sanctity of human life, and so forth. As we read those commandments, we realize that we have broken each and every one of them. That is why the Scripture speaks of the law "that was against us and that stood opposed to us" (Col. 2:14). Because we are lawbreakers, God's law has become our adversary. The list of its regulations is a list of our sins, a record of the infinite debt we owe to God.

God forgave that debt, and the way he did it was by personally nailing it to the cross; "He took it away, nailing it to the cross" (Col. 2:14). What makes this such a vivid image is that it corresponds to the way debts were sometimes cancelled in the ancient world. When a debtor finally paid off all his debts, his creditor would strike a nail through the certificate of debt. In the same way, when Christ died on the cross, God was driving a nail right through the infinite debt of our sin. There are no longer any outstanding charges against us.

Colossians 2 is the chapter Horatio Spafford (1828–1888) had in mind when he wrote the triumphant third verse of the hymn "It Is Well with My Soul:"

> *My sin—O the bliss of this glorious thought!—*
> *My sin, not in part, but the whole,*
> *Is nailed to the cross and I bear it no more;*
> *Praise the Lord, praise the Lord, O my soul!*

The debts we ask God to forgive when we pray the way Jesus taught us to pray are the very debts that were crucified with Christ at Calvary. When Christ died on the cross, all our debts were canceled. The Greek word for "cancel" (*exaleipho*), which Paul uses in Colossians 2, means "to blot out" or "to wipe away." It means that the mountain of debt we once owed to God because of our sin has been completely erased.

In order for Jesus to get rid of our sins this way, he had to meet certain qualifications. This is always the case when a debt needs to be settled. There needs to be what people used to call a "surety," someone to secure the debt, like the co-signer on a loan. Not everyone is able to do this. It has to be someone with good credit. Obviously, the person cannot be a debtor himself; otherwise he would be unable to pay.

Jesus met all the qualifications to stand as our "surety." He was able to settle our debts because he was and is the perfect God-man. His sinless life meant that he did not have any payments to make for his own sins. It also enabled him to offer a perfect sacrifice to God. Because of his divine nature, that sacrifice was of infinite worth. Therefore it was sufficient to pay the full amount of our indebtedness. By the infinite worth of his merits, Jesus canceled the infinite debt of our sin.

Our salvation did not come cheap. The transaction had to be settled in blood, for the Scripture says that "without the shedding of blood there is no forgiveness" (Heb. 9:22b). In order for God to forgive us, Jesus had to pay our debts with his own blood. This he has done, for "in him we have redemption through his blood, the forgiveness of sins" (Eph. 1:7a). Thus the words of the old hymn are true: "Jesus paid it all, all to him I owe."

RENEWING YOUR REPENTANCE

This leaves us with an important practical question: Why do we still need to ask for God's forgiveness? If all our debts have been paid, why do we still need to be pardoned?

It is easy to see why we need to ask God to forgive us at least once. Until we repent for our sins, we are not saved. Therefore, we need to ask God to forgive us our sins, trusting that Jesus died on the cross to cancel all our debts. Yet the Lord's Prayer makes asking forgiveness part of our daily prayers. The fifth petition is joined to the fourth petition by the conjunction "and": "Give us today our daily bread, *and* forgive us our debts" (Matt. 6:11-12 KJV). We need God to "forgive us" as well as to "give us" every day. We are asking him for daily pardon as well as daily provision.

But how can this be? God has already forgiven all our sins once-and-for-all through the death of Jesus Christ. Why then do we need to keep on asking for his forgiveness?

The answer, of course, is that we are not perfect, and never will be in this life. We keep on sinning. We break God's commandments every day, in thought, word, and deed. And although all our sins have been forgiven—past, present, and future—sin still has a way of disturbing our fellowship with God. It interferes with our intimacy with him, estranging us from his holiness. When we sin, therefore, our personal relationship with God needs to be restored. The Puritans called this "renewing our repentance." It means asking God to take the forgiveness he has already granted through Christ's death on the cross and to apply it freshly and directly to our sins.

This is something we need to ask God to do every day. In his book *The Hidden Life of Prayer*, David M'Intyre writes that "Confession of sin should be explicit. . . . When, in the course of the day's engagements, our conscience witnesses against us that we have sinned, we should at once confess our guilt, claim by faith the cleansing blood of Christ, and so wash our hands in innocence."[4]

To understand why we still need to ask for God's forgiveness in this way, it helps to remember that when we confess our sins, we are speaking to our Father. Once we are in Christ, our status as his children is never in jeopardy. But just because he is our Father, we need and want to ask for his forgiveness whenever we sin.

Once, when my son was a small boy, I tried to explain to him why we need the fifth petition of the Lord's Prayer. I said, "If you did something really, really naughty, would I ever throw you out of the house?" The idea sounded so preposterous to my son that he laughed. He knew that his place in his father's heart was absolutely secure. Then I said, "But you would still need to ask for my forgiveness, wouldn't you?" He admitted that he would, because he had learned to prize his fellowship with his father. Jesus prizes fellowship with his Father all the more. Although we are guilty sinners, he wants us to have the same kind of intimacy with the Father that he has, and thus he taught us to pray in these words: "Our Father in heaven . . . forgive us our debts."

For Discussion

1. Have you ever owed a debt (financial, emotional, or a debt of action) to someone? Share how you felt in those circumstances.

2. What are the similarities between financial debt and spiritual debt? What are the differences?

3. In what ways does sin make us indebted to God?

4. When faced with the reality of the enormous debt they owe to God, what are some debt-reduction strategies that people try to apply to their spiritual lives? Why don't those work?

5. What qualifications did Christ's death on the cross have to meet in order for it to pay for our debt? (See Col. 2:13b-14, Heb. 9:22.)

6. Looking at Colossians 2:14, Romans 7:7-11, and Acts 13:38-39, discuss the relationship between God's law and our debt.

7. Psalm 32 describes David's experience of asking for God's forgiveness and being forgiven his debt. Read it now. How does a clearing of our debt enable us to live without deceit (v. 2)?

8. What emotions did David experience as he came to realize his enormous debt of sin in verses 3-4? Have you ever had those same feelings about your sinfulness?

9. What steps did David take to alleviate his debt (vv. 5-6)? Do your times of confession usually contain those same elements?

10. What did David learn about God through his experience of confession and forgiveness?

11. Based on David's experience as recorded in Psalm 32, what are the benefits of confessing our sins?

12. If our debts were paid on the cross, why do we still need to ask for God's forgiveness?

13. How does thinking of your sinfulness in terms of debt change or deepen your understanding of forgiveness?

10

As We Forgive Our Debtors

*For if you forgive men when they sin against you, your heavenly
Father will also forgive you. But if you do not forgive men their
sins, your Father will not forgive your sins.*
MATTHEW 6:14-15

"TO ERR IS HUMAN, BUT to forgive is divine." This common expression
reminds us that God has the capacity to forgive in ways that we do not;
indeed, we find it much easier to commit a sin than to forgive one.

Our difficulties with forgiveness can be illustrated from a moving
episode in the life of Simon Wiesenthal. Wiesenthal was imprisoned in
a Nazi concentration camp in Poland. From there he was sent as part
of a work detail to clean up a hospital for wounded German soldiers.
When he arrived, Wiesenthal was ordered to follow one of the nurses
to a patient's room. There he encountered a dying Nazi, a young S. S.
officer whose badly-burned body was wrapped entirely in bandages.
The man was barely able to speak, yet he wanted to confess his sins
before he died. In particular, he wanted to confess them to a Jew.

The Nazi began to recount his crimes. On one occasion, he had
set fire to a building crammed with hundreds of Jews. When one family tried to escape, he slaughtered them in the street. Tormented by the
memory of their anguished faces, he longed to beg forgiveness from a
Jew before he died. Wiesenthal listened patiently to the man's story.
He recognized that the Nazi's repentance was genuine, yet he was hor-

rified by what the man had done. When the confession was finished, Wiesenthal got up without a word and left the room, unable to offer forgiveness. Yet afterwards he wondered whether or not he had done the right thing. His account of the event closes with this challenge: "You, who have just read this sad and tragic episode in my life, can mentally change places with me and ask yourself the crucial question, 'What would I have done?'"[1]

SINNED AGAINST, AS WELL AS SINNING

Wiesenthal's story shows how hard it is—indeed, how impossible it can be—to forgive. Yet it also shows why forgiveness is so necessary. We live in a cruel world where people do unspeakable things to one another. We are reminded of this every time we use the Lord's Prayer and say "Forgive us our debts, as we also have forgiven our debtors" (Matt. 6:12; cf. Luke 11:4a). From this petition we learn that we are not the only ones in debt. We have debtors of our own, people who owe us something for what they have done to us.

The biblical teaching that explains why there are so many debtors in the world is sometimes called the doctrine of total depravity. Total depravity simply means that the sinful nature goes all the way through every human being. No part of the heart, mind, will, or body is untouched by sin. The Lord's Prayer takes depravity seriously. First it instructs us to pray for our own sins ("Forgive us our debts"). But total depravity does something more than explain what is wrong with us; it also explains what *happens* to us in this sinful world. We sin and are sinned against, so the fifth petition goes on to say, "as we forgive our debtors." Do not be surprised when people irritate and annoy you, or even when they abuse and destroy you. The Bible teaches you to expect that people will wrong you. And sometimes the people who hurt you the most are those you love the most.

There is a danger, of course, in adopting a victim mentality. This is one of the major problems with secular psychology. Some psychologists tell you that whatever is wrong with you is someone else's fault. As a result, some people go through life without ever accepting responsibility for their own actions. Yet the truth is that God holds us responsible for our own actions. Though sometimes victimized, we are not merely victims. No matter what anyone else has done to you, you must live through it and deal with it in a godly way.

There is also a danger in failing to recognize the damage that sin does. This is the major problem with some forms of Christian counseling. Some counselors tell you that whatever is wrong with you is your own fault, that simply repenting for your sins will solve all your problems. As a result, some people go through life blaming themselves for all their struggles. Yet the truth is that we live in a world where we are wounded by sin. Part of what is wrong with us is that we have been wronged by others. God has a way to heal those wounds, a way to ease the pain inflicted by the sins of others. It is called forgiveness. Once God has given us the grace to be forgiven, we also need his grace to be forgiving.

FORGIVEN AND FORGIVING

What is hard to understand about the fifth petition of the Lord's Prayer is the precise connection between our forgiveness and God's forgiveness. That there is a connection is unmistakable. Here is how the *Westminster Shorter Catechism* explains it: "In the fifth petition (which is, *And forgive us our debts, as we forgive our debtors*) we pray, That God, for Christ's sake, would freely pardon all our sins; which we are the rather encouraged to ask, because by his grace we are enabled from the heart to forgive others" (A. 105). In other words, the grace we receive in forgiveness gives us the grace to be forgiving.

Jesus sensed that the fifth petition would be the most difficult for his disciples to understand and apply. So he followed the Lord's Prayer with these words: "For if you forgive men when they sin against you, your heavenly Father will also forgive you. But if you do not forgive men their sins, your Father will not forgive your sins" (Matt. 6:14-15). It was almost as if Jesus said, "Yes, you heard me correctly: 'Forgive us our debts, *as we also* have forgiven our debtors.'"

This is a hard teaching. Yet it is the consistent teaching of Jesus Christ, who said, "Blessed are the merciful, for they will be shown mercy" (Matt. 5:7), and also "Forgive, and you will be forgiven"

(Luke 6:37c). Or again, Jesus said, "When you stand praying, if you hold anything against anyone, forgive him, so that your Father in heaven may forgive you your sins" (Mark 11:25).

The prayer for forgiveness is the only petition in the Lord's Prayer that comes with a condition attached to it. As many theologians have noted, our own forgiveness depends directly on our capacity to forgive. Cyril of Jerusalem (c. 310–386) said, "It is a contract with God when we pray that he may pardon our sins as we forgive our neighbors their debts." Augustine taught the same thing, arguing that in order for us to be forgiven, we must both pray for our sins to be forgiven and forgive the sins of others. Otherwise, we are not forgiven.[2] But we have so much trouble forgiving others that this condition immediately seems to throw our salvation into jeopardy. If we do not forgive, we will not be forgiven. Yet we find it hard to forgive. How, then, can we be forgiven?

There is a famous statement from John Wesley (1703–1791) that illustrates our difficulty. As a young man, Wesley was a missionary to Georgia, where he had a difficult time with the colony's founder, the proud and pitiless General Oglethorpe. During the course of one conversation, the general made this startling comment: "I never forgive." "Then I hope, sir," remarked Wesley, "you never sin."[3] Wesley was thinking of the fifth petition of the Lord's Prayer, which implies that there is no forgiveness for those who never forgive.

There may even be times when this petition turns out to be a request for God *not* to forgive our debts. Charles Spurgeon preached that "unless you have forgiven others, you read your own death-warrant when you repeat the Lord's Prayer."[4] For there are times when we refuse to forgive people, or when our forgiveness is grudging or incomplete. If we then ask God to forgive us the way we forgive others, we are asking him not to forgive us at all! This is why Augustine referred to this part of the Lord's Prayer as "the terrible petition."[5] If we deny forgiveness to our debtors, then we are still in debt ourselves. The unforgiving are unforgiven.

This petition does not mean that our forgiveness is equal to God's. The word "as" joins the two halves of the petition together and draws a comparison between God's forgiveness and our forgiveness. It is only a similarity, however, and not an identity, because God's forgiveness is much greater. The debts he forgives are infinite, while the ones we forgive are relatively small, even if they do not always seem that way to us. There also seems to be something significant about the fact that God forgives our *debts*, while we forgive our *debtors*. The most that we can do is pardon the sinner, not the sin. Only God can clear the actual charges of sin because he alone is the Judge of the universe.

There is something else this prayer does not mean. It does not mean that our forgiveness somehow *causes* God to forgive us. The Scripture says "*as* we have forgiven," not "*because* we have forgiven." Do not be misled by the verb tenses. Grammatically, the *New International Version* is accurate when it puts the second half of the petition in the perfect tense: "Forgive us our debts, as we also *have forgiven* our debtors." Yet this does not mean that our forgiveness comes first, for elsewhere the Bible puts it the other way around: "Forgive as the Lord forgave you" (Col. 3:13).

In the Lord's Prayer, notice which part of the petition comes first. Asking for our own forgiveness takes priority over offering it to others. As William Willimon notes, "Before there is any talk in the prayer about our forgiving anyone else, we are made to ask for forgiveness ourselves. Before there is any consideration of the wrongs that we have suffered, we are made to ponder the great wrong God has suffered through us."[6] The King James Version best captures the logic of the prayer: "Forgive us our debts as we forgive our debtors" (Matt. 6:12).

If we had to forgive before we could be forgiven, then forgiveness would become a work, something we had to do to be saved. Yet we know that salvation comes by grace alone. The only thing required is faith in Jesus Christ, for "everyone who believes in him receives forgiveness of sins through his name" (Acts 10:43). Forgiveness is the free gift of God's mercy to all who believe. We cannot work off our debts, we can only ask for them to be canceled. Therefore, receiving forgiveness has nothing to do with anything we do. In particular, our capacity to forgive others does not make us somehow eligible for God's forgiveness. However, if we refuse to forgive others, then we are disqualified from receiving forgiveness ourselves. Unforgiveness is unforgivable. The Puritan Thomas Watson wrote, "Our forgiving others is not a cause of God's forgiving us, but it is a condition without which he will not forgive us."[7]

The ability to forgive is one of the surest signs of having been forgiven. It is part of the proof that we have received God's grace. This idea lies behind the paraphrase of the fifth petition in the *Heidelberg Catechism:* "Forgive us just as we are fully determined, as evidence of your grace in us, to forgive our neighbors" (A. 126). Those who are truly forgiven, truly forgive. The sins they commit are of greater importance to them than the sins they suffer.

If we have an unforgiving spirit, however, it shows that we have not taken to heart what it means to ask for and to receive forgiveness. In the words of Kent Hughes, "If I refuse to forgive, there can be only one reason, and that is that I have never understood the grace of Christ. I am outside grace, and I am unforgiven."[8] The great English poet George Herbert (1593–1633) explained why this must be so: "He that cannot forgive others, breaks the bridge over which he himself must pass if he would ever reach heaven; for every one has need to be forgiven."[9]

THE UNMERCIFUL SERVANT

To help explain the relationship between our forgiveness and God's forgiveness, Jesus told a story about a man who owed an enormous debt. He was a servant in the royal palace and he owed the king ten thousand talents, which would be millions in today's economy. Since the servant was unable to pay, the king ordered the man and his entire family to be sold into slavery in order to repay the debt. At this, the servant fell on his knees and pleaded for the king's forbearance. "Be patient with me," he begged, "and I will pay back everything" (Matt. 18:26). The king took pity on his servant, canceled his debt, and let him go.

After the servant left his audience with the king, he chanced upon another servant who owed him some money. The debt was not insignificant, yet it paled in comparison to what he had owed the king. Nevertheless, the servant seized his debtor by the neck and began to choke him. "Pay me back!" he shouted. At this, the other servant fell to his knees and begged for more time. In fact, he used nearly the same words his fellow servant had used at the king's throne just moments before: "Be patient with me, and I will pay you back" (Matt. 18:29). But the servant refused to forgive his debtor. Instead, he had the poor man dragged off to prison!

Before recounting what happened next, it is worth pausing to notice how many similarities there are between this story and the fifth petition of the Lord's Prayer. The story and the prayer both deal with the forgiveness of debts. The story began with a man who owed the king more than he could pay. When the man asked for mercy, the king canceled his debt. This is what we ask for when we pray, "Forgive us our debts." Because of our many sins, we owe an infinite debt to God our King. But when we ask for his mercy, he cancels our entire debt. He does this because Jesus paid it all when he died on the cross for our sins.

Notice also that the king's forgiveness has the priority. He forgives first. Nor is his forgiveness based on anything the servant has done, least of all his ability to forgive others. The only reason the king forgives is because he is merciful. In the same way, God's forgiveness comes before our forgiveness. His mercy is what enables us to forgive in the first place.

Sadly, the servant in the story found himself unable to forgive. We are bound to conclude from this that he had never truly entered into the heart of the king's mercy. His own repentance was insincere. He asked for forgiveness without knowing what forgiveness really involved. He begged for his debt to be canceled without understanding how much he actually owed. When the time came to forgive his debtor, therefore, he was unable to say, "I forgive you." And since he was unable to forgive, he was unable to be forgiven. The story ends with the king treating this unmerciful servant exactly the way he deserved—not with forgiveness, but with fury. When the king heard what had happened, he called the man in and said, "You wicked servant. . . . I canceled all that debt of yours because you begged me to. Shouldn't you have had mercy on your fellow servant just as I had on you?" (Matt. 18:32-33). Then he sent the poor man off to prison to be tortured until he could pay back all his debts.

This is a warning that merely repeating the words of the Lord's Prayer is not enough. It is possible to use these petitions without any real hope of ever having them answered. Even the unmerciful servant could mumble the fifth petition of the Lord's Prayer, or at least words to the same effect. Yet his unwillingness to forgive proves that he had no idea what he was asking for. In the end he was unforgivable.

FORGIVE YOUR DEBTORS

The meaning of this parable is obvious. Jesus explained it to his disciples by saying, "This is how my heavenly Father will treat each of you unless you forgive your brother from your heart" (Matt. 18:35). It is either forgive or perish. God has forgiven the infinite debt of your sin. Now you must forgive anyone who sins against you. Otherwise, you prove that you have never received forgiveness in the first place, that you are still in God's debt and therefore liable to the perfect severity of his justice.

If we must forgive, then how shall we do it? What does it mean to forgive our debtors?

It means to forgive everyone for everything. Forgive the neighbor who backed over your begonias. Forgive the sibling who colored in your books and the parent who never showed you much affection. Forgive the spouse who doesn't meet your needs and the child who ran away from home. Forgive the co-worker who stabbed you in the back and the boss who denied your promotion. Forgive the church member who betrayed a confidence, or the pastor who gave you poor spiritual care. Forgive people for whatever they have done to you.

If you are a Christian, you do not have the right to withhold forgiveness from anyone for anything. The Bible says, "Forgive each other, just as in Christ God forgave you" (Eph. 4:32). To forgive, therefore, is to imitate God. It is to follow the example of Jesus, who even forgave his enemies while he was dying on the cross (Luke 23:34). In Christ there is grace to forgive the greatest sinners, from the uncle who molested you to the drunk driver who killed your son.

Forgiving our debtors means forgiving them even if they do not ask for our forgiveness. Debtors do not always know how much they are in your debt. Sometimes they know, but they don't care, and all you end up receiving is a half-hearted apology, or maybe no apology at all. This is why there is such a big difference between forgiveness and reconciliation. It takes two to reconcile, so it is not always possible to be reconciled. But it takes only one to forgive. So if people do you wrong, forgive them, whether or not they ask for forgiveness. You cannot cancel their sin. Only God can do that, and he will only do it if they repent. But what you can do is set aside your own anger, bitterness, and resentment towards them. In other words, you can forgive them.

Forgiving our debtors means forgetting as well as forgiving. Sometimes it proves impossible to forget completely, of course. There are also times when it is necessary to hold people accountable for their actions. But what I mean by forgetting is not holding on to a grudge. Forgiveness has to do with the attitude of your heart, and forgiveness that refuses to forget is no forgiveness at all. It is like the man who said he buried the hatchet, but then left the handle sticking up out of the ground. That is not forgiveness at all. True forgiveness means "laying down our right to remain angry and giving up our claim to future repayment of the debt we have suffered."[10] It means giving up my right to hurt you for what you have done to me.

Forgiving our debtors also means learning how to say, "I forgive you." Not "that's okay" or "don't worry about it," but "I forgive you." When someone asks for your forgiveness, it means that he has committed a sin. Forgiveness is the only response that calls sin a sin. Sin should not be overlooked, covered up, or ignored. It should be faced and forgiven.

Forgiving our debtors means forgiving them over and over again. Jesus told his story about the unmerciful servant because Peter was trying to set limits on forgiveness. He thought seven times was about the most that one person should or even could be forgiven. But Jesus said, "I tell you, not seven times, but seventy-seven times" (Matt. 18:22). In other words, forgiveness has no limits.

This suggests that forgiveness is often a process, particularly when the wounds are deep. What seems like full forgiveness at one time may later prove to have been incomplete. The thing to do in that case is to forgive all over again, and to continue to forgive as often as necessary. Like the rest of the Lord's Prayer, this petition is for everyday use. Since people sin on a daily basis, forgiveness is a part of daily life.

Offering someone such radical forgiveness is not easy. It is not easy to forgive everyone for everything, to forget as well as to forgive, or to keep on forgiving over and over again. Forgiveness is costly, and the more someone has hurt you, the harder it is to forgive. It helps to remember that we ourselves are debtors, and that therefore our forgiveness flows from God's forgiveness. If you have been forgiven, you can and must forgive others as well as you can. You can forgive because God—who has forgiven all your debts in Jesus Christ—gives you the grace to forgive. You *must* forgive because it is vital to your own spiritual health.

Forgiveness brings great joy, not only to the forgiven, but especially to the forgiver. The Greek term for "forgiveness" (*aphiemi*) comes from a word that means "to let go." Forgiveness is a release, a letting go of self-destructive feelings such as anger, bitterness, and revenge. Those attitudes poison intimacy with God and harmony with human beings. The only antidote for these poisonous attitudes is forgiveness. In his book *Forgive and Forget*, Lewis Smedes writes, "There is one right word for the amazing moment when we release a person who dug a deep hurt into our lives. The right word for this is not acceptance, it is not tolerance, it is not excusing, it is not forgetting, it is not covering up. The right word is forgiveness. And when you release the other person you also lift a tremendous burden from yourself."[11]

Mission founder Richard Wurmbrand once met a man who had experienced the divine release that comes through forgiveness. Wurmbrand was in a Communist prison in Romania at the time, lying in a prison cell reserved for those who were dying. In the cot on his right was a pastor who had been beaten so badly that he was about to die. On his left was the very man who had beaten him, a Communist who was later betrayed and tortured by his comrades.

One night the Communist awakened in the middle of a nightmare and cried out, "Please, pastor, say a prayer for me. I have committed such crimes, I cannot die." The pastor feebly sat up and called for another prisoner to help. Slowly, he stumbled past Wurmbrand's cot and sat at the bedside of his enemy.

As he watched, Wurmbrand saw the pastor begin to caress the hair of the man who had tortured him. Then he spoke these amazing words: "I have forgiven you with all of my heart and I love you. If I who am only a sinner can love and forgive you, more so can Jesus who is the Son of God and who is love incarnate. Return to Him. He longs for you much more than you long for Him. He wishes to forgive you much more than you wish to be forgiven. You just repent." There, in the prison cell, the Communist began to confess all his murders and tortures. When he had finished, the two men prayed together, embraced, and then returned to their beds, where each died that very night.[12]

The pastor had learned how to forgive. He had learned how to forgive everyone for everything, even those who had wounded him most. He had learned how to forgive and forget, how to forgive over and over again. He had learned all this from Jesus, who first forgave his own debts, and then taught him to forgive his debtors.

For Discussion

1. Share an experience when it was hard to forgive.

2. Why is it so hard to forgive people?

3. Read Matthew 6:14-15, Mark 11:25, and Colossians 3:13. What is the connection between God's forgiveness of our sins and our forgiveness of others?

4. Knowing the close connection between our forgiven-ness and the way we forgive others, why might the fifth petition of the Lord's Prayer be a dangerous one for us to pray?

5. In what ways, other than the extent of forgiveness, is human forgiveness different from God's forgiveness?

6. Jesus told a story that helps us better understand the relationship between our forgiveness of others and God's forgiveness of us. Read it in Matthew 18:21-35. How does this story enhance your understanding of the fifth petition of the Lord's Prayer?

7. How is the king in this story like God? In what ways is God different from this king?

8. What does the fact that the servant was unwilling to forgive the debt owed him tell you about the servant?

9. What truths about forgiveness are illustrated in the conclusion of this story (vv. 32-34)?

10. Looking especially at verses 21-22 and 35, what warnings does this parable hold for us?

11. What are some characteristics of true forgiveness? See Matthew 5:44-45, Colossians 3:12-13, and Ephesians 4:31-32 to get you started.

12. In what ways does reconciliation go beyond forgiveness?

13. How can understanding the difference between our forgiveness and God's make it easier to forgive others?

14. How does forgiving others benefit the forgiver? Describe the sense of relief you felt when you finally forgave someone.

15. Spend time in prayer this week asking God to enable you to forgive those who have wronged you.

11

Lead Us Not into Temptation

Pray that you will not fall into temptation.
LUKE 22:40

HE HEARD IT IN THE middle of the night. Long before the first rays of sun pierced the eastern horizon he heard the sound that shattered his soul. It was only a shriek from the barnyard, the cry of an old rooster, but to his ears it must have sounded like the devil himself, crowing in triumph. For when Peter heard that noisy old bird, he "remembered the word Jesus had spoken: 'Before the rooster crows, you will disown me three times'" (Matt. 26:75).

Jesus was right: thrice Peter denied his master. First, while he was sitting in the courtyard of the high priest, a servant girl accosted him, saying "You also were with Jesus of Galilee" (Matt. 26:69b). Peter said he had no idea what she was talking about, but just to be safe he went out to the gateway, where he promptly disowned Jesus again. When they asked him a third time, "he began to call down curses on himself and he swore to them, 'I don't know the man!'" (Matt. 26:74). Thus a night that began with feasting ended in profanity—desperate lies salted with the curses of an old sailor. Immediately, the rooster crowed, and Peter went out to weep bitter tears.

Jesus knew it would come to this. He had even prophesied that it would happen. But there is a sense in which it was all unnecessary. Peter did not have to deny his master. There was a way for him to stand firm in his faith, a way for him to resist temptation, as there always is. Peter would have had the courage to stand if only he had remembered to pray the way Jesus taught him to pray! When you pray, Jesus said, pray like this: "Lead us not into temptation" (Matt. 6:13a). In case Peter had forgotten that petition, which he had learned a few years earlier, Jesus reminded him of it that very night. When they were together in the Garden of Gethsemane, he said, "Pray that you will not fall into temptation" (Luke 22:40).

A REAL TEMPTATION

Sadly, Peter did not utter that prayer in the garden. He went to sleep instead. So when the temptation came, he fell right into it. His downfall shows that the sixth petition of the Lord's Prayer is crucial for the Christian life. Thomas Aquinas (1224–1274) said, "The Lord's Prayer contains all that is to be desired and all that we ought to avoid."[1] And the main thing we ought to avoid, of course, is sin. Having prayed for our food ("Give us this day . . .") and for our forgiveness ("Forgive us our debts . . ."), we must also pray about our frailty ("Lead us not into temptation . . ."). Our sins are forgiven, we know, but we are likely to sin again. We stand in mortal danger of sinning against our Savior, the way Peter did.

We are in this mortal danger for two reasons. First, our enemy is strong. He is deadly strong, for our adversary is Satan himself. This is clear from the second half of the petition: "Lead us not into temptation, but deliver us from the Evil One" (Matt. 6:13). And who is "the evil one," if not the devil himself, the one the Scriptures call "the tempter" (Matt. 4:3; 1 Thess. 3:5)?

Satan was Simon Peter's adversary, too. One of the reasons Peter fell was because his enemy was too strong for him. "Simon, Simon," said Jesus, not long before his betrayal, "Satan has asked to sift you as wheat" (Luke 22:31). The Evil One wants to sift us as well, to toss us into the sieve of temptation and shake us out.

Consider what a powerful enemy Satan is. Peter himself later described him as a "roaring lion" who "prowls around . . . looking for someone to devour" (1 Pet. 5:8). The devil is relentless. No sooner have we resisted one temptation than his demons come after us with another. He is persistent. If we show the slightest sign of weakening, he will keep pressing us until we sin. He is crafty, gradually leading us down the road of destruction. He starts with a small temptation. When it succeeds, he presents us with a slightly greater temptation, slowly drawing us deeper and deeper into sin. He is subtle, so subtle that sometimes we find ourselves sinning before we are even aware of being tempted.

Satan is also creative. He offers us a complete line of transgressions to choose from: greed, lust, hatred, despair, and anger. Then there are all the refined sins, the sins that only religious people commit like self-righteousness and spiritual pride. Sometimes our enemy changes tactics, suiting the temptation according to age and circumstance. Small children are tempted to be selfish. I am reminded of a little girl who was tempted to steal a cookie from the cookie jar. "Sometimes the devil tempts me," she said, "and sometimes he tempts me good!" Adolescents are tempted to be sarcastic. Young people are tempted to be sexually immoral. As they grow older, people are tempted to be greedy or bitter or fearful. If Satan cannot get us to sin one way, he will tempt us to sin another.

The devil is also deceptive. He lies about the true nature of sin. "You really need to do this," he says. "Just this once." "You can't help yourself." "It's not going to hurt anybody, so who cares?" "You know you are going to give in eventually, so go ahead and sin now, just to get it over with." "It will make you feel good!" With these and a thousand other falsehoods, the tempter goes about his deadly business. When Satan tempts you next, how will he do it? What strategy will he adopt?

You are in mortal danger because your enemy is strong. Satan is not infinitely strong, because he is a finite being and thus is unable to tempt everyone all the time. He has plenty of helpers, however, which means that at this very moment an adversary is plotting your spiritual downfall. There is an "Evil One" who wants to discredit your testimony, divide your family, and destroy your ministry.

The second reason you are in mortal spiritual danger is that you are weak. You are a sinner; therefore, sin is a real temptation for you. You are as prone to fall into it as Peter was, if not more so. We know we are weak because the Bible tells us so. Biblical history is all about weak sinners falling to temptation. The German scholar Ernst Lohmeyer wrote:

> We might call the Bible, Old and New Testaments, the 'Book of Temptations'. On its first pages stands the temptation of the first man and woman, and on its last the prophetic descriptions of the great temptation which is 'coming on the whole world, to try those who dwell on the earth' (Rev. 3.10). Between this beginning and this end there stretches the history of the people of God and with it the histories of individual men of God, and this single history, too, is a continuous chain of temptations . . . which has gone on since the world was created and will go on until it ends.[2]

The apostle Paul said, "These things . . . were written down as warnings for us. . . . So, if you think you are standing firm, be careful that you don't fall!" (1 Cor. 10:11-12). The weaknesses we see in the people of the Bible are the very weaknesses we ought to recognize in ourselves. Like Eve, who ate the forbidden fruit, we are vulnerable to temptation when we act on our own. Like Abraham, who lied about his wife to save his neck, we are vulnerable to temptation when we are scared. Like David, who slept with Bathsheba while his men were off to war, we are vulnerable to temptation when we are idle. Like Elijah, who wanted God to end his life, we are vulnerable to temptation when we are exhausted. Like Peter, who denied his Lord even after he promised to die for him, we are vulnerable to temptation when we are overconfident. In other words, we are vulnerable to temptation practically all the time.

Our weakness explains why so many of our experiences with temptation involve failure. For most of us, it is easier to think of times we have fallen to temptation than to think of times we have stood firm. We are rather like Mr. Doolittle in the musical *My Fair Lady*. Mr. Doolittle is an immoral old man who explains that "The Lord above gave liquor for temptation, to see if man would turn away from sin." "But," he sings, "with a little bit o' luck, with a little bit o' luck, when temptation comes you'll give right in!"

That little song describes our spiritual condition apart from Christ. When temptation comes, we give right in. No Christian can withstand temptation in his or her own strength: not the teacher giving the Sunday School lesson; not the dear old woman praying for all the missionaries; and certainly not the minister standing in the pulpit. Nor can any group of Christians withstand temptation in their own strength: not the congregation wearing its Sunday best; not the school founded on solid biblical principles; and not even the family worshiping around the dinner table. Temptation is too dangerous for us to handle on our own, in part because it comes from our own evil desires (James 1:14).

HOW TO RESIST TEMPTATION

If we are so weak, and our enemy so strong, is there anything we can do to withstand temptation? There are many ways to try and resist it. One is to let someone else know that you are facing temptation. Ask a Christian brother or sister to pray for you, to counsel you, and to hold you accountable not to give in to a particular sin.

Another way to resist temptation is to avoid all known occasions of sin. This is what Joseph did when Potiphar's wife wanted to have intercourse with him. He not only refused to go to bed with her, but he refused to be alone with her at all (Gen. 39:10). He stayed out of a situation that was bound to lead him into sin. In the same way, if you are tempted to play the slot machine, stay off the bus that goes to Atlantic City. If you are tempted to share some gossip, unplug the telephone.

When you do face temptation, you can defeat it by quoting Scripture. This is what Jesus did when he was tempted by the devil in the wilderness (Matt. 4:1-11). He knew a Bible verse for every temptation. Thus he used the Word of God, "the sword of the Spirit" (Eph. 6:17), to strike a mortal blow against sin.

In the same way, we should study and memorize what the Scripture says about our favorite sins. If you are tempted to engage in sexual sin, then learn Job 31:1: "I made a covenant with my eyes not to look lustfully at a girl." If you tend to procrastinate, then memorize this proverb: "A sluggard does not plow in season; so at harvest time he looks but finds nothing" (Prov. 20:4). When you are tempted to complain, quote Paul's testimony to the Philippians: "I have learned the secret of being content in any and every situation, whether well fed or hungry, whether living in plenty or in want. I can do everything through him who gives me strength" (Phil. 4:12b-13). Martin Luther found this kind of practical memory work to be extremely helpful for his own spiritual growth. He said, "I have had great troubles of mind; but so soon as I laid hold on any place of Scripture, and stayed myself upon it as upon my chief anchor, straightway my temptations vanished away."[3]

Those are all good ways to fight against temptation. But there is something else that must come first. Before getting a brother or sister to help, before avoiding the occasions of sin, before fighting back with Scripture, we must pray the way Jesus taught us to pray. The very first thing to do in our struggle against sin, long before we even face temptation, is to pray for God to deliver us. That is why we need the last petition of the Lord's Prayer. We need to pray for our spiritual protection. If we could resist temptation in our own strength, this prayer would be unnecessary. But we cannot always resist. Thus we must ask God to do what we cannot do for ourselves, and that is to keep us from temptation. In the words of Thomas Watson, "Prayer is the best antidote against temptation."[4]

PRAYING AGAINST TEMPTATION

What does it mean to ask God not to lead us into temptation? What, exactly, are we praying for?

The Greek word for "lead" means to bring forcefully. It is like a teacher who grabs one of her students by the ear and "leads" him to the principal's office. At first glance, it almost seems as if God is to blame for our temptations. If we are asking God *not* to lead us into temptation, that implies that sometimes he does lead us there. And if God leads us into temptation, then he must be the one who tempts us. Right?

Obviously, that cannot be right. The Bible clearly teaches that God does not tempt anyone. "When tempted, no one should say, 'God is tempting me.' For God cannot be tempted by evil, nor does he tempt anyone" (James 1:13). God never tries to get anyone to do evil. Yet the fact that he does not tempt us does not mean that our temptations are somehow outside his control. God is sovereign over all the affairs of life, including every temptation to sin. Although he does not cause our temptations, he does allow them to occur.

Perhaps the best place to see the part God plays in temptation is the testing of Christ in the wilderness. The Bible says that "Jesus was led by the Spirit into the desert to be tempted by the devil" (Matt. 4:1). Notice that Jesus was not tempted by his Father. The devil was the one who did the tempting. Nevertheless, the whole situation was under the Father's control. God's Spirit led God's Son into the desert to be tested. Thus Jesus was led by the Spirit, but tempted by the devil. The same is true in the Christian life. God allows his people to be tempted, even though he does not do the tempting. As the Puritans often taught, God "permits sin, but does not promote it."[5]

We are beginning to understand what it means to ask God not to "lead us" into temptation. Although God does not tempt us, he does allow us to be tempted. But what, exactly, is meant by temptation? The Greek word for "temptation" can mean "test," "trial," "temptation," or even "tribulation." Those meanings are all closely related, of course, but they need to be kept distinct.

Consider the difference between a test and a temptation. Every temptation is a kind of test, but not every test is a temptation. Tests and temptations have different purposes, and they come from different places. Tests are designed to show what someone can do. Their purpose is positive, which explains why God himself tests people, as he tested Abraham (Heb. 11:17). A test is a trial posed by God to prove the strength of our faith. Temptations, on the other hand, are more negative. Their explicit purpose is to entice people to sin, which is why they come from the Evil One. A temptation is a trial posed by Satan, with the wicked hope that we will fail.

So what did Jesus have in mind when he taught his disciples how to pray—testing, temptation, or both? Martin Luther taught that the Lord's Prayer had to do with testing in general, and not simply with temptation.[6] More recently, the Church of England voted to eliminate temptation from the Lord's Prayer altogether, replacing it with this petition: "Save us from the time of trial."[7]

One problem with this view is that testing is a good and necessary part of the Christian life. We are strengthened by testing, and therefore we are to rejoice in it: "Consider it pure joy, my brothers, whenever you face trials of many kinds, because you know that the testing of your faith develops perseverance" (James 1:2-3). Not only are we to rejoice in testing, we are even to pray for it. "Test me, O LORD, and try me" (Ps. 26:2), prayed King David. If the Lord's Prayer is about testing, rather than temptation, then it almost seems to contradict other Scripture. Why would Jesus tell us not to ask for something that will do us so much good?

A slightly different interpretation takes this petition to refer to one trial in particular; namely, the final tribulation at the end of history. After all, that is the way the Greek word for testing is used near the end of the Bible: "Since you have kept my command to endure patiently, I will also keep you from the hour of trial that is going to come upon the whole world to test those who live on the earth" (Rev. 3:10). The sixth petition, then, would be a prayer for salvation from the coming judgment. Tom Wright translates it like this: "Let us escape the great tribulation, the great testing, that is coming on all the world."[8]

One advantage of this interpretation is that it makes good sense of the second half of the petition ("Deliver us from the Evil One") by looking forward to Satan's final and absolute defeat at the end of history. If that is what Jesus had in mind, however, he undoubtedly would have made his meaning more clear. At the very least, he would have used the definite article, calling it "*the* testing." Yet he said simply, "Lead us not into temptation."

It seems best, therefore, to retain the traditional meaning of "temptation." The sixth petition may include tests and trials of various kinds, but primarily it refers to temptation to sin. When we pray, therefore, we are to ask God to keep us from being tempted. This part of the Lord's

Prayer means something like this: "Do not lead us into temptation, Lord; on the contrary, keep us as far away from it as possible."

Sometimes, in his mercy, God answers this prayer by keeping us from being tempted at all. Often, however, God *does* allow us to be tempted. Therefore, "Lead us not into temptation" must be something more than a request not to be tempted. Among the first to realize this was Origen, who pointed out that if we ask not to be tempted at all then we are asking God for the impossible, since we cannot avoid being exposed to all kinds of temptation. What we are really asking, therefore, is for God to save us when we are tempted. Origen explained it like this:

> Unless the Saviour is bidding us pray for impossible things, it seems to me worth inquiring how we are bidden to pray that we do not enter into temptation, when the whole life of men upon earth is a time of temptation. . . . Let us therefore pray to be delivered from temptation, not by not being tempted (for this is impossible), but by not being overcome when we are tempted.[9]

An old Jewish prayer may help to explain what Jesus meant. The prayer comes from the Talmud, and it may date back nearly to the time of Christ himself. It goes like this:

> *Lead my foot not into the power of sin,*
> *And bring me not into the power of iniquity,*
> *And not into the power of temptation,*
> *And not into the power of anything shameful.*[10]

Jesus was saying much the same thing when he taught us how to pray against temptation. God may not keep us from being tempted at all, but he can keep us from falling under temptation's power. Thus we are to pray that God will spare us from those satanic attacks that we are unable to withstand. "Do not let us be overcome by temptation, Lord!" "Protect us from being drawn into sin!" "Keep us from succumbing to Satan!"

By praying this way, we acknowledge both our own weakness and the strength of our enemy. We admit how likely we are to fall into sin.

Yet we beg that God will not allow us to do so, that he will keep us from being tempted beyond what we can bear. We pray that God will not abandon us, but will send us the help of the Holy Spirit. We trust him to be faithful to his promise that "he will not let you be tempted beyond what you can bear. But when you are tempted, he will also provide a way out so that you can stand up under it" (1 Cor. 10:13).

To summarize, in the Lord's Prayer we not only pray for God to *prevent* us from being tempted—which sometimes is impossible—but also to *preserve* us when we are tempted. The *Westminster Shorter Catechism* brings both meanings together when it says: "In the sixth petition (which is, *And lead us not into temptation, but deliver us from evil*) we pray, That God would either keep us from being tempted to sin, or support and deliver us when we are tempted" (A. 106).

TEMPTED IN EVERY WAY

We may be sure that God will answer this prayer. God answers all our prayers one way or another. But we have special reasons to believe that he will answer our prayer not to be led into temptation.

One reason God will answer this prayer is that he answered it when Jesus prayed it. We see this in the Garden of Gethsemane, where Jesus told Peter and the other disciples—twice—to pray that they would not fall into temptation (Luke 22:40, 46). Jesus told them to pray because he knew from his own experience that prayer is the best way to combat temptation. He not only told his disciples to pray, but he also prayed himself. In the hour of his last temptation, the temptation not to endure the saving sufferings of the cross, Jesus was at prayer in the garden. The same God who gave Jesus the strength to withstand his temptations will give us strength to face our temptations, if we ask him.

Another special reason that God will hear our prayer is that Jesus knows all about our temptations and can explain them to his Father. "For we do not have a high priest who is unable to sympathize with our weaknesses, but we have one who has been tempted in every way, just as we are—yet was without sin" (Heb. 4:15). Jesus has experienced every last one of our temptations. He experienced them without ever giving in to them, which is why he was able to offer a perfect sacrifice for our sins. Now, whatever the temptation, Jesus can say, "Been there; resisted that." Having experienced all our temptations, Jesus is able to sympathize with our weakness. According to Thomas Watson, "he is so sensible of our temptations as if he himself lay under them, and did feel them in his own soul."[11] Since he understands our temptations, Jesus understands what we mean when we pray, "Lead us not into temptation." He not only understands that prayer, he repeats it, for even now he stands at the right hand of the Father, interceding for us to be preserved from temptation.

We may be sure, therefore, that when we pray "Lead us not into temptation," God will answer our prayer. For we are using a petition taught and proven by our Lord Jesus, a petition he comprehends and communicates to the Father. "Let us then approach the throne of grace with confidence, so that we may receive mercy and find grace to help us in our time of need" (Heb. 4:16).

Charles Spurgeon once told the story of a man who received mercy and found grace in his time of need. The story comes from the days of the English Reformation. It has been retold by Kent Hughes, who writes:

> History records the fate of two men who were condemned to die in the burning days of Queen Mary. One of them boasted very loudly to his companions of his confidence that he would stand firm at the stake. He did not mind the suffering; he was so grounded in the Gospel that he knew he would never deny it. He said that he longed for the fatal morning even as a bride for the wedding.
>
> His companion in prison in the same chamber was a poor trembling soul who could not and would not deny his Master; but he told his companion that he was very much afraid of the fire. He said he had always been very sensitive to suffering, and he was in great dread that when he began to burn, the pain might cause him to deny the truth. He besought his friend to pray for him, and he spent his time in very much weeping over his weakness and in crying to God for strength. The other continually rebuked him and chided him for being so unbelieving and weak.

When they both came to the stake, he who had been so
bold recanted at the sight of the fire and went back ignomin-
iously to an apostate's life, while the poor trembling man
whose prayer had been *"Lead me not into temptation"* stood
firm as a rock, praising and magnifying God as he was burnt
to a cinder.[12]

It was the man who knew his own frailty who glorified God. He
knew that he was weak, that his enemy was strong, and that only God
could save him. So he did what Jesus told Peter to do when he was in
danger of denying his Lord. He prayed, "Lead me not into temptation," and God answered his prayer.

For Discussion

1. Imagine that you are visiting the United States for the first time.
   Based on the advertising on TV, what would you say are some of the
   most prevalent temptations offered by the culture?

2. Why are we so easily tempted that we need to pray for protection
   against temptation? What is it about Satan that makes him so dangerous to us?

3. Read Genesis 3:1-7. What do the serpent's questions tell us about
   how Satan tempts us?

4. What mistakes did Eve make that opened her to temptation?

5. What further tempted Eve in verse 6? What temptations in today's
   culture appeal to those same senses?

6. What are some situations in which you are likely to be tempted?
   What physical or emotional conditions make you vulnerable to
   temptation?

7. What are some specific ways that an understanding of Satan's temptation tactics can help you avoid giving in to temptation?

8. Look at what Joseph did when he was tempted by Potiphar's wife in Genesis 39:10. What wise action did he take to resist temptation?

9. Jesus withstood temptation by using Scripture (Matt. 4:1-11). Read the passage. For each temptation, discuss what lay behind that temptation and why giving in to it would have been sinful.

10. How does each passage Jesus uses effectively counter the temptation?

11. What other methods, besides fleeing from it and using Scripture to combat it, can you use to fight against temptation?

12. Why does God allow us to be tempted? See Deuteronomy 8:2 to guide your thinking.

13. James 1:13-14 tells us that God does not tempt us. How can you reconcile that truth with the sixth petition of the Lord's Prayer?

14. What do you think is the difference between a test and a temptation? Read James 1:2-4, 12 and 1 Peter 4:12-14 for information on the tests God sends to us.

15. The sixth petition of the Lord's Prayer refers to temptation, not tests or trials. Knowing that truth, describe what this petition means in your own words. A helpful question to keep in mind is, "What are we not requesting by praying this prayer?"

16. God has promised in 1 Corinthians 10:13 that he will never let us be tempted beyond what we can bear. How might knowing that truth help you the next time you are tempted?

17. Memorize a verse or two that will help you in an area in which you are particularly tempted. For example, if you struggle with lust, you might memorize Job 31:1. If you tend to worry, you might memorize Philippians 4:19.

12

Deliver Us from the Evil One

*The Lord is faithful, and he will strengthen and
protect you from the Evil One.*
2 THESSALONIANS 3:3

LATE ONE NIGHT A COUPLE came home from a dinner party. The husband dropped his wife off at their doorstep in Center City, Philadelphia and went to look for a parking space. (Their home did not have a garage.) As he was parking, just a few blocks from home, the man noticed three tough-looking strangers walking straight towards his car. Sensing that he might be in danger, he decided to wait for the men to walk past. When they were about a block away, he felt safe enough to step out of his car. Immediately, the men turned around and began to stalk him.

The man's first impulse was to prepare for a fight, especially since he was trained in the martial arts. But his next impulse was even stronger, and that was to pray for God to deliver him. He could tell that his pursuers were gaining on him, and they would catch up to him before he reached home. Yet he had a supernatural sense of peace, knowing that God had heard his prayer and would protect him from evil. By the end of the block, his enemies were right behind him. He turned the corner sharply and there, right in front of him, were a half-dozen men hard at work unloading a moving van. His would-be assailants stopped at the corner, hesitated, and then moved on.

As you can imagine, the man praised God for his deliverance. When he arrived home his wife was waiting for him at the door. He did not want to alarm her, so he didn't say anything about the incident. But when he mentioned it the next morning, she said, "Aha, that explains it!" She then related how, while waiting for him to return from parking the car the night before, she had experienced an overwhelming urge to pray for his protection. When he walked through the door two minutes later, safe and sound, she didn't know what to make of it. Now they both knew that God had answered their prayers by delivering them from evil.

WHO (OR WHAT) IS THE EVIL ONE?

We live in an evil world, so the last thing we ask in the Lord's Prayer is for God to deliver us. When you pray, Jesus said, this is how you should do it: "Deliver us from the Evil One." Some scholars consider that phrase to be a petition unto itself, which would give the Lord's Prayer seven petitions in all. Others consider it part of the sixth petition ("Lead us not into temptation"). However one divides the prayer, it is clear that both phrases belong together: "Lead us not into temptation, but deliver us from the Evil One." The word "but" ties both requests together and shows the contrast between them. Not only do we ask God to keep us from evil, but we also ask him to rescue us when evil comes. Thus it is good to pray that God will keep you out of the lions' den; however, if you find yourself there, keep praying for him to deliver you!

This petition proves, incidentally, that God will not keep us from ever being tempted. The fact that we must pray for his deliverance shows that we will sometimes fall into temptation. Herman Witsius explained it like this: "A Christian ought to pray daily to his Heavenly Father that he may not be led into temptation, but that, when temptation does occur, he may courageously resist evil."[1] Remember, too, the words of the *Westminster Shorter Catechism*, "That God would either keep us from being tempted to sin, or support and deliver us when we are tempted" (A. 106).

Notice that the Bible does not say simply "Deliver us from evil."

That is how the King James Version expresses it, and thus it is the way many people recite the Lord's Prayer. However, most modern translations say, "Deliver us from the Evil *One*," which is more accurate. It does raise the question, however, as to which "Evil One" Jesus had in mind.

In the Greek language, "Evil One" can refer to an evil thing. That is the way Paul used the term when he wrote to Timothy: "The Lord will rescue me from every evil attack and will bring me safely to his heavenly kingdom" (2 Tim. 4:18a). Thus, the "Evil One" could be any evil event or circumstance, which is the way Martin Luther understood it. "Under this heading," Luther wrote, "we count strife, famine, war, pestilence, plagues, even hell . . . in short, everything that is painful to body and soul."[2] When we pray, therefore, we are asking God to deliver us from all evil. We are praying for him to do something more than save us from temptation; we are asking him to save us from any and every evil thing.

Another possibility is that "Evil One" refers to an evil man. An "Evil One" is any person who rebels against God. This idea comes up frequently in the Old Testament, especially in the psalms of David. "Deliver me from evildoers" (Ps. 59:2a); "Rescue me, O LORD, from evil men" (Ps. 140:1a). There were times when Jesus spoke this way as well. He used the expression earlier in his Sermon on the Mount, when he said, "Do not resist an evil person" (Matt. 5:39). What Jesus literally said was "Do not resist an Evil One."

Yet behind everything and everyone evil there stands an even greater evil—the devil himself. Most often, when the New Testament speaks of "the Evil One," it is speaking of Satan. There is an example of this in the Sermon on the Mount. Jesus said, "Simply let your 'Yes' be 'Yes,' and your 'No,' 'No'; anything beyond this comes from the Evil One" (Matt. 5:37)—that is, Satan. There are other examples throughout the New Testament. It is "the Evil One" who snatches away the good seed of God's Word (Matt. 13:19), who sows weeds next to God's wheat (13:38-39), who has to be resisted with the shield of faith (Eph. 6:16), and so forth (2 Thess. 3:3; 1 John 2:13; 5:18).

In the Lord's Prayer there are two small grammatical details which help to confirm that Satan is the Evil One.[3] Jesus taught us to pray to be delivered *from* the Evil One. Ancient Greek had two prepositions meaning "from." One was used with impersonal objects, as in the sentence "I got this book from the library." The other preposition was nearly always used for persons: "I got this book from Bob." The preposition used in the last petition of the Lord's Prayer is the one that takes a personal object. In other words, we are asking to be delivered from a person and not from a thing. When Jesus tells us further that this person is "*the* Evil One," it seems clear that he is speaking of the devil.

Do you believe in the personal existence of Satan? Jesus certainly did. After all, he had faced his direct diabolical attacks in the wilderness (Matt. 4:1-11). Having withstood the full force of those temptations, Jesus taught his disciples to pray against the Evil One whenever they prayed. Unless we believe in the reality of the devil, we will not see the need to pray against him. Nor will we be able to understand the nature of evil. Evil is not a mysterious cosmic force, a kind of supernatural "dark side." On the contrary, behind every evil thing there is a malignant, malevolent being who hates God and all his creatures. Therefore, we cannot consider evil without confronting the Evil One.

In the bitter aftermath of World War II, the German theologian Helmut Thielicke observed that "there is a dark, mysterious, spellbinding figure at work. Behind the temptations stands *the* tempter, behind the lie stands *the* liar, behind all the dead and bloodshed stands *the* 'murderer from the beginning.'" Thielicke went on to say "Dear friend, in our times we have had far too much contact with demonic powers."[4]

It is from these dark powers that we need to be delivered. To "deliver" is to lead someone out of danger, the way God led the children of Israel out of slavery in Egypt. When you pray, you are asking God to rescue you from all the attacks of Satan. You are praying that when you face evil—as you must—God will lead you out of it. In his exposition of the Lord's Prayer, Witsius offers this helpful summary:

> *To be delivered from evil* does not mean to be so preserved by divine power that we may not afterwards fall into any sin, or that we may never be exposed to the assaults of the Devil. Our condition in this world does not allow this. But it denotes that

gracious government of Divine Providence, by which the more powerful and formidable attacks of the Devil are prevented, or the necessary supplies of strength administered to us, that we may not yield or be overcome.[5]

THE HISTORY OF THE EVIL ONE

If we are not to be overcome by the Evil One, we must be aware of two dangers. One is to minimize Satan's importance by failing to recognize that he has real spiritual power. The other danger is to exaggerate his importance, becoming spellbound by his sinister schemes.

C. S. Lewis (1898–1963) wrote a book about demons called *The Screwtape Letters*. In the introduction he observed that "There are two equal and opposite errors into which our race can fall about the devils. One is to disbelieve in their existence. The other is to believe, and to feel an excessive and unhealthy interest in them. They themselves are equally pleased by both errors, and hail a materialist and a magician with the same delight."[6] The devil is a deceiver who "masquerades as an angel of light" (2 Cor. 11:14). He wants to make us believe that he doesn't exist. As the French poet Charles Baudelaire (1821–1867) once wrote, "The devil's cleverest ruse is to make men believe that he does not exist."[7] Or to give us the false impression that he is a silly old character in a red suit with little horns and a forked tail. Or to convince us that his devilish powers are so overwhelming that we are helpless to resist. The best way to counter these diabolical lies is with biblical truth. What does the Bible teach about the Evil One?

The biography of Satan begins in heaven, where he was created to serve as one of God's most beautiful angels. After a time Satan rebelled against the King of Heaven. He refused to give God the glory because he wanted all the glory for himself. Therefore, God cast him down from heaven (Rev. 12:13; cf. Luke 10:18). From that time forward, the Evil One vowed to hate God and to loathe him forever. Ever since, he has tried to destroy God's work, particularly God's special plan to save the people he made in his image.

Satan began by tempting Adam and Eve in the Garden of Eden. He lied to the woman, telling her that eating the forbidden fruit would make her godlike (Gen. 3:5). By persuading her to sin, he also brought death to the human race. But almost as soon as humanity fell into sin, God promised to send a Savior who would bring Satan to absolute ruin:

> *"I will put enmity*
> *between you and the woman,*
> *and between your offspring and hers;*
> *he will crush your head,*
> *and you will strike his heel."*
>
> GENESIS 3:15

As Satan slithered away from the garden, he determined to do everything in his power to stop the Savior from ever coming. All through the Old Testament, he tried to kill off the seed of the woman. Cain murdered Abel. Ishmael hated Isaac. Esau contended against Jacob. Saul tried to assassinate David. It was all part of the Evil One's desperate attempt to abort God's plan of salvation. As Donald Grey Barnhouse explained in his exposé of Satan, *The Invisible War*, "Satan's enmity against mankind is, in reality, an enmity against God because God has been pleased in His sovereign grace to plan salvation through the Word made flesh; and Satan's primal hatred is, therefore, Christ. His hatred of mankind was, first, a racial hatred, blindly attempting to destroy all men that he might blot out the line of the promise."[8]

Satan failed. In the fullness of time, the Savior God promised was born of a virgin. Having failed to prevent his coming, the only thing Satan could do was try to keep him from accomplishing his saving purpose. So the Evil One went out into the wilderness. There he tempted Jesus to use his deity to his own advantage, to win the kingdom without enduring the cross.

Jesus resisted every temptation, of course. Yet the Scripture says that "when the devil had finished all this tempting, he left him until an opportune time" (Luke 4:13). Afterwards, we see him skulking in the shadows of the Gospels, looking for a chance to get rid of Jesus once and for all. He tried to seize the opportunity when Jesus first told his disciples about his crucifixion and resurrection. "Never, Lord!" said Peter, but the Evil One was at work, for "Jesus turned and said to Peter,

'Get behind me, Satan!'" (Matt. 16:23). Satan took another chance when Judas Iscariot grew tired of waiting for God's kingdom. The Bible says that Satan entered Judas. Then Judas, possessed by the devil, went to the Jewish authorities and offered to betray Jesus (Luke 22:3-4; cf. John 13:27). The Evil One worked his plan to perfection. In rapid succession, Jesus was betrayed, arrested, beaten, crucified, and buried.

Except the plan didn't work after all, for Jesus rose from the dead. The most Satan could do was bruise the Savior's heel. By his resurrection, Jesus gained a crushing victory over sin, death, and the devil.

THE STRATEGIES OF THE EVIL ONE

The Evil One has not given up the fight, however. Having failed to defeat Christ, he now tries to defeat the Christian. To quote again from Herman Witsius:

> That wicked enemy is so inveterately opposed to the Divine majesty that he would gladly, if it were possible, overturn the throne of God. As he utterly despairs of accomplishing that object, he throws out all his venom against the elect, employs every expedient, and exhausts all his devices to enslave those whom the power of God has torn from his grasp. . . . He assaulted the first Adam in Paradise. . . . He made an attempt on the second Adam in the wilderness, but his efforts were foiled. Disappointed in that expectation, he bends all his attack on those whom Christ has claimed to be his own.[9]

Since the Evil One is our most hateful enemy, we should beware of his tactics. The Bible teaches that when Satan "saw that he had been hurled to the earth," he "went off to make war against . . . those who obey God's commandments and hold to the testimony of Jesus" (Rev. 12:13, 17). As he continues to wage this invisible war, he has many weapons at his disposal.

First, there is *domination*. Satan is the dominator. The Bible teaches that sinners who have not yet come to faith in Christ are "under the power of the devil" (Acts 10:38; cf. 26:18). By serving themselves, rather than serving God, they are actually serving Satan.

Whether they realize it or not, he "has taken them captive to do his will" (2 Tim. 2:26b). Anyone who is not a child of God is a child of the devil (1 John 3:10; cf. John 8:44; 1 John 3:8a). Apart from Christ, therefore, the human race is dominated by the Evil One. Wherever there is greed, deception, hatred, or violence, the devil has established his deadly dominion. He "leads the whole world astray" (Rev. 12:9), holding individuals, families, institutions, nations, and whole civilizations under his power. He even holds the power of death (Heb. 2:14)—at least spiritually, if not physically.

Another weapon of the Evil One is *temptation*. Satan is the tempter (1 Thess. 3:5). Of all the weapons at his disposal, temptation is perhaps the oldest and the most effective. It is the weapon Satan used against Eve in the Garden of Eden. It is the weapon he uses so often today, enticing people to look at the pornographic image on the computer screen, to covet the merchandise in the catalog, or to envy someone else's success.

Once we have fallen to temptation, the Evil One resorts to *accusation*. Satan is the accuser, the one who charges God's children with being unfaithful to their Father. The Bible calls him "the accuser of our brothers, who accuses them before our God day and night" (Rev. 12:10b). This is what Satan did to Joshua the high priest in the vision of Zechariah (Zech. 3:1-7). Joshua stood before God's heavenly throne dressed in filthy clothes, signifying his sin. Satan stood right beside him to accuse him before God of being a filthy sinner. He does the same thing to us, accusing us of unrighteousness so that we despair of ever standing in God's righteous presence.

Then there is *confrontation*, by which I mean all the ways the Evil One opposes the Christian church. Satan stages a continual confrontation with the work of the Gospel. He is the adversary, for that is what his very name means. Satan confronts the church by teaching error. He corrupts ministers and seminaries with unsound doctrine. He fools people into believing the false gospel of health and wealth. Some people seek signs and wonders, but according to the Bible, the work of *Satan* is often "displayed in all kinds of counterfeit miracles, signs and wonders, and in every sort of evil that deceives those who are perishing" (2 Thess. 2:9b-10a). The adversary hinders the work of missions. There were many occasions when he opposed the apostle Paul: he schemed against him (2 Cor. 2:11; cf. Eph. 6:11); he tormented his flesh (2 Cor. 12:7); he stopped him from traveling to Thessalonica (1 Thess. 2:18). There were even times when Satan had the early Christians put into prison (Rev. 2:10).

We must be careful not to give the Evil One more credit than he deserves. Some people think, for example, that every time a missionary's computer crashes it is the work of the devil (actually, Satan is probably more interested in how the missionary *responds* to the crash than he is in the crash itself). But the devil can only do what God allows him to do. Remember that Satan had to get God's permission before he could touch Job's person or property (Job 1:10-12; 2:4-6). The Evil One is not infinite. He is neither omnipotent nor omnipresent. Therefore, he cannot do everything he wants to do or be everywhere he wants to be.

Satan is dangerous, however. He is the dominator, the tempter, the accuser, and the adversary. And these are only some of what John Calvin called "the violent assaults of Satan."[10] From the very beginning of the world, the Evil One has done everything in his power to destroy God's plan for his people. Sooner or later, everyone is bedeviled by one or more of his weapons. Hence our need for the Lord's Prayer, in which we beg God to deliver us from evil.

DELIVERANCE!

There are times when evil cannot be escaped, when the only hope is deliverance. A good example of such a deliverance comes from British history.

> In the old English wars between the king and Parliament, the town of Taunton, attacked by Lord Goring and defended by Robert Blake, sustained a long siege. Food rose to twenty times its market value. Half the houses were blown down by a storm of fire, and many of the people perished from hunger. Through all of this, the townsfolk had been accustomed to meet in St. Mary's Church to pray, and we may be sure that the burden of

their daily prayers to the Father was, "Deliver us!" One day as
they were assembled for this purpose, hoping to hear that the
enemy had at last retreated, a trusty messenger came to the
church door and spoke but one word, "Deliverance!" In a
moment the magic word flew through the vast assembly, and
all shouted with one voice, "Deliverance!"[11]

Deliverance! It is what God has guaranteed in his Gospel. We cannot withstand Satan in our own strength, but God has promised to
lead us out of danger and save us from all the powers of evil. For the
Scripture says that "the Lord is faithful, and he will strengthen and
protect you from the Evil One" (2 Thess. 3:3). Therefore, we do not
deny the existence of evil. Nor do we seek to avoid it at all costs.
Rather, we trust God to deliver us from it.

It was this trust in divine deliverance that led Martin Luther to
write his great hymn about Christ's triumph over Satan, *"Ein' Feste
Burg"* ("A Mighty Fortress"):

> And though this world, with devils filled,
>   should threaten to undo us,
> We will not fear, for God hath willed his truth
>   to triumph through us.
> The prince of darkness grim, we tremble not for him;
> His rage we can endure, for lo! his doom is sure;
>   one little word shall fell him.

The little word that dooms the devil is the Gospel. The Gospel of
salvation from sin through the crucifixion and resurrection of Jesus
Christ is the word of deliverance. It is the good news God first
announced in the Garden of Eden, that Satan's head would be crushed
by the woman's seed (Gen. 3:15). Jesus is the Seed born to deliver us
from the Evil One. The Bible teaches that "the reason the Son of God
appeared was to destroy the devil's work" (1 John 3:8b).

How did Jesus deliver us? He defeated the devil by dying on the
cross and rising again from the dead. His plan was that "by his death
he might destroy him who holds the power of death—that is, the
devil" (Heb. 2:14b). When Jesus died on the cross, he paid the full

penalty for our sins. When he rose from the dead, he gained victory over the grave. Therefore, by his crucifixion and resurrection, Jesus has saved us from sin and death. What this means is that he has undone the work of the devil. Satan can no longer hold God's children under the power of sin and death.

As we have seen, the Evil One still has many weapons in his arsenal—domination, temptation, accusation, confrontation. But our crucified and risen Savior has a countermeasure for every demonic attack.

The Evil One tries to dominate, but Jesus liberates, saving us from the devil's dominion. "For he has rescued us from the dominion of darkness and brought us into the kingdom of the Son he loves" (Col. 1:13; cf. Acts 26:18). If you still find yourself dominated by the devil, doing Satan's will rather than God's will, then you need to be delivered from evil. Pray for Jesus to save you from the Evil One.

The Evil One tries to tempt us, but Jesus gives us the power to resist temptation. He showed us how to do it when he defeated the devil in the wilderness (Matt. 4:1-11). As we learned in the previous chapter, Jesus resisted temptation by prayer and the Word of God. Now he tells us to do the same thing: "Resist the devil, and he will flee from you" (James 4:7).

The Evil One tries to accuse us, but Jesus defends us with his own record. When Satan charges that we are sinners, Jesus stands before his Father's throne and says, "They may be sinners, but I died for their sins." He holds out his hands to show how he was pierced for our transgressions, and then he covers our unrighteousness with his own righteousness. "Therefore, there is now no condemnation for those who are in Christ Jesus" (Rom. 8:1).

The Evil One tries to confront the church, but Jesus is the church's rock and foundation. One of the last things he prayed before his crucifixion was, "Protect them from the evil one" (John 17:15). As the church preaches and lives the Gospel, God answers that prayer. Even as Christians face hardships, opposition, persecution, and martyrdom, God is building his church, and the gates of hell will not prevail against it (Matt. 16:18).

Soon the battle will be over. It will not be long now before the day will come when Satan will no longer trouble us. There will be no more domination, temptation, accusation, or confrontation. Our warfare will be over and our commander, Jesus Christ, will call us away from the battlefield to receive the victor's crown.[12] Then we will share in his absolute, eternal conquest of the Evil One. For the Bible promises that "the God of peace will soon crush Satan under your feet" (Rom. 16:20a). Then the devil will be thrown into the lake of fire that God has prepared for him (Matt. 25:41), and in which he "will be tormented day and night for ever and ever" (Rev. 20:10).

What more can we ask than the total defeat of evil and the Evil One? Cyprian said that "when we say, Deliver us from evil, there remains nothing further which ought to be asked. When we have once asked for God's protection against evil, and have obtained it, then against everything which the devil and the world work against us we stand secure and safe."[13] Safe and secure we will remain, invincible in Christ for all eternity.

For Discussion

1. Have you ever had an experience where you actually feared for your life? Share your story with the group.

2. How would you define or illustrate the word *evil* to someone who had never heard it before?

3. How do you think this petition is related to the one you studied in the last chapter—"and lead us not into temptation?" Why are they in the order they are?

4. What stories or pictures do you associate with the concept of deliverance? How might those types of images change the way you pray this petition of deliverance from evil?

5. Why is it dangerous to either disbelieve or obsess about Satan? What negative effects have you seen from these two errors?

6. Read Acts 10:38. What weapon of Satan is mentioned in this verse? What are the implications of the fact that those who have not accepted Jesus' forgiveness for their sins are under Satan's power?

7. In 1 Thessalonians 3:5, we learn that Satan is the tempter. What temptations seem to be especially effective in contemporary culture or in your own life?

8. Revelation 12:10b tells us that Satan is our accuser. What are the effects of his accusations in the lives of believers?

9. What weapons do believers have against Satan's power, temptations, accusations, and opposition? See Ephesians 6:10-18 to get you started.

10. Read 2 Thessalonians 2:9-10. According to this passage, what are some of the ways Satan opposes the Christian church? Can you think of any other ways Satan is fighting against the church today?

11. In addition to understanding the strategies Satan uses against believers, it is important to keep in mind that God is still in control of everything that happens. What are some of Satan's limitations? Job 1:10-12 and 2:4-6 will give you some hints.

12. If the opposite errors of ignoring and fearing Satan are both dangerous, what is the appropriate attitude of the believer toward Satan? See 2 Thessalonians 3:3 to help you start thinking about this question.

13. What promises do we have in the Bible that give us encouragement when we see the Evil One at work? Give Scripture references if you can.

14. How has your study of evil and deliverance changed the way you think about and pray the last petition of the Lord's Prayer?

13

The Power and the Glory

Yours, O LORD, is the greatness and the power and the glory
and the majesty and the splendor, for everything in heaven
and earth is yours. Yours, O LORD, is the kingdom;
you are exalted as head over all.
1 CHRONICLES 29:11

IN THE PREVIOUS CHAPTER, we recounted the history of the Evil One, tracing the tragic story of his fall from glory to his descent into hell. As we come to the end of the Lord's Prayer, one further detail from Satan's biography deserves our attention. It comes from the great confrontation in the wilderness between Jesus and the devil, which Luke describes as follows: "And the devil, taking him up into an high mountain, shewed unto him all the kingdoms of the world in a moment of time. And the devil said unto him, All this power will I give thee, and the glory of them: for that is delivered unto me; and to whomsoever I will give it. If thou therefore wilt worship me, all shall be thine" (Luke 4:5-7, KJV).

Do you see what Satan was doing? He was trying to claim the kingdom and the power and the glory for himself. First he showed Jesus the kingdoms of the world in all their glory. Then he said that he had the right to hand those glorious kingdoms over to Jesus. In other words, Satan claimed to hold the power of the kingdom and the glory.

Jesus promptly told the devil to get lost: "Thou shalt worship the Lord thy God, and him only shalt thou serve" (Luke 4:8b, KJV). That is also how Jesus taught us to pray, by ascribing worship to God alone, for to him alone belongs the kingdom, to him alone belongs the power, and to him alone belongs the glory. With these words, prayer gives way to praise and the Lord's Prayer ends, not with another petition, but with a doxology: "For thine is the kingdom, and the power, and the glory, forever. Amen" (Matt. 6:13b, KJV).

A BIBLICAL DOXOLOGY

Christians have prayed these words for nearly two thousand years, yet there is some question as to whether they were part of the original Lord's Prayer or not. In the *New International Version*, the prayer closes with the words "deliver us from the Evil One" (Matt. 6:13). There is a note in the margin to explain that some late manuscripts also include the words "for yours is the kingdom and the power and the glory forever. Amen."

The actual situation is somewhat complicated. None of the western manuscripts of Matthew's Gospel, which were written in Latin, contain a doxology. This probably explains why early church fathers like Tertullian, Cyprian, and Augustine (from the second, third, and fourth centuries, respectively) were unfamiliar with what has since become the traditional ending of the Lord's Prayer. The situation was different in the east, however, where the biblical manuscripts were written in Greek. Nearly all the eastern manuscripts of Matthew *do* include the doxology, although it is missing from some early texts. It is also missing from the Gospel of Luke in which the Lord's Prayer ends rather abruptly with the words, "And lead us not into temptation" (Luke 11:4b).

What other evidence exists? There is the version of the Lord's Prayer found in a Christian writing called *The Didache*, which was probably written early in the second century. The prayer in *The Didache* does contain a doxology, although in a slightly different form because it leaves out the kingdom; it simply says, "for thine is the power and the glory for ever."[1] On the basis of this somewhat contradictory evidence, it seems best to conclude that the traditional doxology possibly was not part of the original text of Matthew, but certainly was in use from the early days of the church.

It is not hard to guess why the doxology might have been added. Jewish prayers of that time nearly always ended with words of praise. For example, each of the standard synagogue prayers—known as the "Eighteen Benedictions"—ended with a doxology. The most common Jewish doxology went as follows: "Blessed be the name of the glory of his kingdom for ever and ever."[2] It would have been unthinkable for a Jew to offer a prayer in those days without some kind of doxology, especially a prayer that ended the way the Lord's Prayer ended, with the words "Deliver us from the Evil One." Rather than letting the Evil One have the last word, it must have seemed only natural to close with praise to God. It is even possible that the reason Jesus did not give his disciples a doxology on this occasion (if, in fact, he did not) was because they were already accustomed to praying this way. In all likelihood, they always ended their petitions with a doxology. One scholar suggests that "Jesus must have intended that the Our Father should conclude with a doxology, but would have left the user to fill it in for himself."[3]

All of this still leaves us with a practical question, however: What should we do when we pray? Should we use the traditional doxology or not? Based on his study of the ancient texts, the Renaissance scholar Erasmus of Rotterdam (c. 1469–1536) opposed using the doxology and condemned "the rashness of those who do not hesitate to append their own trifles to a divine prayer."[4] More recently, John Broadus has written, "Surely it is more important to know what the Bible really contains and really means, than to cling to something not really in the Bible, merely because it gratifies our taste, or even because it has for us some precious associations."[5]

These warnings are valuable because they remind us not to add anything to Holy Scripture, which is perfect in every way. Yet it hardly seems right to consider the traditional ending to the Lord's Prayer a mere trifle or a matter of taste, for it is a highly appropriate way for the prayer to end. The doxology is satisfying to the soul. Kent Hughes calls it "the song of the heart that prays after the Lord's pattern of prayer."[6] It is also enlightening to the mind. The Puritan commentator Matthew Henry (1662–1714) showed how the doxology relates to the rest of the Lord's Prayer. We pray "Thy kingdom come" because we know that God rules the kingdom. We pray "Thy will be done" because we know that God has the power. And we pray "Hallowed be thy name" because we know that God is the glory.[7]

The most important thing, however, and really the only thing that matters, is that this doxology is biblical. What could be more biblical than ascribing the kingdom, the power, and the glory to God? This is the language of so many New Testament doxologies:

> *Now to the King eternal, immortal, invisible, the only God, be honor and glory for ever and ever. Amen.*
>
> 1 TIMOTHY 1:17

> *God, the blessed and only Ruler, the King of kings and Lord of lords, who alone is immortal and who lives in unapproachable light, whom no one has seen or can see. To him be honor and might forever. Amen.*
>
> 1 TIMOTHY 6:15B-16

> *The Lord will rescue me from every evil attack and will bring me safely to his heavenly kingdom. To him be glory for ever and ever. Amen.*
>
> 2 TIMOTHY 4:18

> *To the only God our Savior be glory, majesty, power and authority, through Jesus Christ our Lord, before all ages, now and forevermore! Amen.*
>
> JUDE 25

> *You are worthy, our Lord and God, to receive glory and honor and power.*
>
> REVELATION 4:11A

> *To him who sits on the throne and to the Lamb be praise and honor and glory and power, for ever and ever!*
>
> REVELATION 5:13B

In these and many similar passages, God is given praise for his kingdom, his power, and his glory.

Then there is the prayer that matches the traditional ending of the Lord's Prayer most closely of all. It is the prayer King David offered when God's people presented their offerings for building the temple:

> "Yours, O LORD, is the greatness and the power
> and the glory and the majesty and the splendor,
> for everything in heaven and earth is yours.
> Yours, O LORD, is the kingdom;
> you are exalted as head over all."
>
> 1 CHRONICLES 29:11

Therefore, whether it was spoken by Jesus or not, the traditional ending of the Lord's Prayer is part of the biblical pattern for prayer. When you pray, it is right and good to give God the glory for the power of his kingdom.

YOURS, O LORD, IS THE KINGDOM

First we praise God for his kingdom, declaring that he is ruler over all. David said, "Yours, O LORD, is the kingdom" (1 Chron. 29:11b). What makes his prayer especially significant is that David was a king in his own right, the greatest king of Israel. Furthermore, he offered his prayer during one of his greatest moments. It had long been on David's heart to build God a house, a glorious temple for the ark of the covenant. God did not allow David to build the temple—which was a task for his son Solomon to carry out—but he did allow him to gather the materials for its construction. At David's request, all the people brought their offerings to Jerusalem: gold and silver, bronze and iron, wood and stone, marble and precious gems.

This amazing display of wealth would have filled most kings with pride, but when David saw the riches of his kingdom, he was overwhelmed with gratitude to God. He stood before his people, raised his hands in prayer, and said:

"Yours, O LORD, is the kingdom;
  you are exalted as head over all.
Wealth and honor come from you;
  you are the ruler of all things."
1 CHRONICLES 29:11B-12A

David acknowledged that his kingdom was actually God's kingdom, that he was not so much a royal king as he was a loyal subject.

It is not easy for the kings of this world to worship God as king. One thinks of Nebuchadnezzar, who praised himself for the power, the glory, and the majesty of Babylon. Or of Caesar Augustus, who, according to the ancient historians, was concerned with nothing but "the interests of the Empire and the myth of his own glory."[8]

Kings are not the only ones who have this problem, however. We sense the same attitude in the contemporary church, searching for a bigger and better ministry, striving to increase its market share, and scheming to garner more political power. If only Christians had control of Congress, people say, then all would be right with the world!

This is our personal problem as well. Like Satan, we want to dethrone God and take the kingdom for ourselves. We want power, so we can control our own destinies. We want authority, so we can make people do what we want. We want wealth, so we can buy more things and experience more pleasures. That is exactly why we need the Lord's Prayer. For it is when we pray that we remember who the real King is. We get down on our knees, bow before his throne, and say "Yours, O Lord, is the kingdom."

We have prayed about the kingdom before. Near the beginning of the Lord's Prayer, we learned about the plan, the purpose, and the progress of God's kingdom (see chapter 6). God's plan is to establish his kingdom through the preaching of the cross. His purpose is to rule in the hearts of his people. The progress of this spiritual kingdom will be steady, but slow. In one sense, the kingdom has already come with the death and resurrection of Jesus Christ. It continues to grow as his cross and his empty tomb are preached in all the world. There is another sense, however, in which we are still looking for the kingdom, waiting for the king to come again. We live in the kingdom of grace, where Christ rules by faith, but we wait for the kingdom of glory, when Christ will reign supreme over all.

The doxology at the end of the Lord's Prayer mentions the kingdom again, only this time it says something slightly different. Back in the second petition, we prayed for the kingdom to come. In the doxology, we acknowledge that God is *already* the King. As Jesus once said to his disciples, "The kingdom of God is among you" (Luke 17:21b, alternative reading). Jesus is the King; where he is, the kingdom is. Therefore, what the Lord's Prayer says is simply a fact: "Thine *is* the kingdom." Even now, Jesus sits at the right hand of God, in the place of absolute authority over earth and heaven.

At the same time that we pray for God's kingdom to come in all its fulness, we praise God that he is already the King. Here, at the end of the Lord's Prayer, we acknowledge God as sovereign over everything in heaven and earth. We claim Jesus as our own king, the ruler of our thoughts, actions, and emotions.

As we pray, his kingdom comes. For when we pray "Thine is the kingdom," God establishes his rule over our prayers, and thus over our hearts. In his little study of the Lord's Prayer, Joachim Jeremias writes, "Where men dare to pray in the name of Jesus to their heavenly Father with childlike trust, that he might reveal his glory and that he might grant to them already today and in this place the bread of life and the blotting out of sins, there in the midst of the constant threat of failure and apostasy is realized, already now, the kingly rule of God over the life of his children."[9]

YOURS, O LORD, IS THE POWER

Every king has power, but not every king has as much power as he would like. The kingdoms of this world are all limited monarchies. Their economies are limited by their natural resources. Their armies are limited by the strength of their military personnel. Their policies are limited by the wisdom of their counselors. But the kingdom of God does not have any of these limitations. The King who reigns above is the Lord God Almighty. His power is absolute, for "the Lord God omnipotent reigneth" (Rev. 19:6, KJV). Hence we pray, as David prayed, "Yours, O Lord, is the power."

A whole book could be written on the power of God. He is omnipotent, all-powerful, the God of infinite strength and might. We could discuss his power over creation, the way he made all things out of nothing. We could explore his power over history, the way all things come to pass according to the will of his eternal decree. We could analyze his power over sin and death, the way he conquered them both through the cross and the empty tomb. We could testify to his power over life, the way his Spirit transforms everyone who comes to faith in Christ.

There is one kind of divine power, however, that seems especially important here at the close of the Lord's Prayer, and that is God's power to answer prayer. We depend on that power for each and every one of our petitions. We pray, "Our Father which art in heaven, hallowed be Thy name." By doing so, we trust that God has the power to hallow his name, to show by the worship of angels and humans that he is the holy, holy, holy God. We pray, "Thy kingdom come," trusting that through the preaching of the Gospel and the conversion of sinners, God's Spirit will spread God's rule through all the earth. "Thy will be done," we pray, "on earth as it is in heaven." Then we wait for God to work out his purpose, believing that he has the power to do whatever he wills.

Having prayed for God's name, God's rule, and God's will, we begin to pray for our own needs. We know that God has the power to provide food, clothing, and shelter, so we pray "Give us this day our daily bread." Then we trust him to provide everything we need, the same way he provided what David needed for God's temple. We ask God to "Forgive us our debts," trusting that he has the power to take away our sin through the cross of Christ. Last of all, we pray for God to deliver us from the temptations of the Evil One, and thus to show his absolute power over the devil.

When we pray the way Jesus taught us to pray, we pray for many things. Helmut Thielicke once said, "Great things, small things, spiritual things and material things, inward things and outward things—

there is nothing that is not included in this prayer."[10] What gives us the confidence to make all these requests? The power of the Almighty God.

The omnipotence of God is what we confess every time we say, "For thine is . . . the power." The word "for" establishes the connection between the rest of the Lord's Prayer and the doxology. It grounds our petitions in our praise. First comes our long list of requests. On what basis do we expect God to grant them? *"For* thine is the power." What we pray for is based on the attributes of the God to whom we pray. The reason we pray for God's glory and for our good is because we know that God is able to answer our prayers. Indeed, he "is able to do immeasurably more than all we ask or imagine, according to his power" (Eph. 3:20a). The phrase "Thine is the power" is a statement of our faith. It acknowledges our utter dependency on divine grace for everything we need, and it expresses our absolute confidence in God's ability to hear us and to help us.

YOURS, O LORD, IS THE GLORY

Once we have been brought into God's kingdom and have seen his power, the only appropriate way for us to respond is by giving him the glory. America's greatest theologian, Jonathan Edwards (1703–1759), once set out to explain God's glory in a work called "The End for Which God Created the World."[11] Edwards pointed out that the word "glory" is used several different ways in the Bible.[12] The word comes from the Hebrew term for "heavy," and thus "signifies gravity, heaviness, greatness, and abundance." When we speak of the glory of God, we refer first to the internal weight of God's character. Glory is the "excellency, dignity, and worthiness" of God. It is not so much a divine attribute in itself as it is the cumulative weight of all God's attributes. Glory is the gravity of God's being.

God does not keep the weight of his glory to himself, however, which brings us to a second meaning of the word. "Glory," wrote Edwards, "is also the outshining of the internal greatness or excellence. The word 'glory' is used in Scripture often to express the exhibition, emanation, or communication of the internal glory. Hence it often signifies an effulgence, or shining brightness, by an emanation of beams of light."[13] In other words, God sometimes reveals his inward nature through outward displays of his majesty, ordinarily in a dazzling display of light. Think of what Moses experienced when he met God on the mountain (Exod. 33:12-23); of what Isaiah experienced in the temple when he saw the Lord high and lifted up (Isa. 6:1-5); or of what the disciples encountered on the Mount of Transfiguration (Matt. 17:1-5). What these men experienced were visible manifestations of God's invisible majesty. God revealed to them the sparkling splendor of his divine being.

The most spectacular display of God's glory is through his Son, Jesus Christ. God the Son became a man so that we could see the glory of God. He revealed God's glory in many ways, but especially by suffering and dying on the cross for our sins. In his death and resurrection, Jesus made the most amazing display of God's love and justice, demonstrating the glory of God in the salvation of sinners.

The reason Jesus saved us was so that we would glorify God. This is the third way the Bible speaks of glory. First, glory is the inward majesty of God; second, it is the brightness God sometimes shines out into the world; third, it is the worship we offer to God. When we see God's glory, the proper way for us to respond is to give him the glory— to offer him all the honor and praise he deserves. As Edwards concluded in his book, "The end of the creation is that the creation might glorify [God]. Now what is glorifying but a rejoicing at that glory he has displayed?"[14]

To God alone be the glory! This is the essence of true religion. It was the motivation behind the Reformation. Indeed, it is the motivation behind any true Christianity. Consider the example set by the Tarascan Indians of Mexico. According to the missionary Maxwell Lathrop, many Tarascan Christians refer to themselves as *doxistas*. They take this name from the New Testament word *doxa*, which means glory. A *doxista* is someone who lives for the glory of God. It is simply another way of defining a Christian, for a Christian is someone who glorifies God, not only in this life, but for all eternity.

FOREVER AND EVER, AMEN!

"Yours is the kingdom and the power and the glory forever"—this traditional doxology is a fitting way to end the Lord's Prayer. Calvin called it a "firm and tranquil repose for our faith."[15] It lifts our minds and hearts to the glorious throne where God rules the universe with grace and power. Thus our prayer ends where it began, by giving worship to God alone.

The *Westminster Shorter Catechism* ends the same way. Its last answer summarizes the doxology from the Lord's Prayer: "The conclusion of the Lord's prayer (which is, *For thine is the kingdom, and the power, and the glory, for ever, Amen*) teacheth us to take our encouragement in prayer from God only, and in our prayers to praise him, ascribing kingdom, power, and glory to him. And, in testimony of our desire, and assurance to be heard, we say, *Amen*" (A. 107).

This brings us to the very last word of the Lord's Prayer. The word is "amen," the Hebrew word that means "I agree," or "so be it." It is a word Jesus often used, not only to pray, but especially to verify the truth of what he was saying. "Amen, amen," he would say. In the *New International Version*, this is paraphrased as "I tell you the truth" (e.g., John 10:1, 7). More literally, "Amen" means "verily, verily," or "truly, truly." It is a way of testifying that something is true. As Martin Luther once said, "it is a word uttered by the firm faith of the heart," a word used to affirm "something that is most certainly true."[16]

The "Amen" at the end of the Lord's Prayer is not an afterthought. In a way, it is the most important word in the whole prayer, because it makes the prayer our own. When we say "Amen," we add our personal endorsement to what someone else has prayed. The Lord's Prayer is often used in public worship. Sometimes the congregation recites the prayer in unison. On other occasions, a worship leader may offer it on behalf of the congregation. But either way, the congregation affirms the entire prayer by saying "Amen" once it is over. "Yes, Lord, this is our prayer, and we mean it with all our hearts."

William Willimon and Stanley Hauerwas of Duke University recount a story that illustrates the power of the "Amen" at the end of the Lord's Prayer:

In a prison camp in World War II, on a cold, dark evening after a series of beatings, after the hundreds of prisoners of war had been marched before the camp commander and harangued for an hour, when the prisoners were returned to their dark barracks and told to be quiet for the rest of the night, someone, somewhere in one of the barracks began saying the Lord's Prayer. Some of his fellow prisoners lying next to him began to pray with him. Their prayer was overheard by prisoners in the next building who joined them. One by one, each set of barracks joined in the prayer until, as the prayer was ending with, "Thine is the kingdom, the power, and the glory," hundreds of prisoners had joined their voices in a strong, growing, defiant prayer, reaching a thunderous, "Amen!"[17]

That is a picture of what we do when we pray the way Jesus taught us to pray. We offer our prayers from the barracks, for we are still at war with our old enemy, the devil. Soon our warfare will be over and Christ will reign victorious. But in the meantime it is cold and dark, and we must take courage by praying together. At the end of our prayers, we give God the glory for the power of his eternal kingdom. Whatever precise words we use, this is the biblical way to pray.

Charles Wesley took the traditional conclusion and turned it into verse. His words provide a fitting doxology for our study of the Lord's Prayer:

> *Yea, Amen! Let all adore thee,*
> *High on thine eternal throne;*
> *Saviour, take the power and glory:*
> *Claim the Kingdom for thine own:*
> *O come quickly!*
> *Alleluia! Come, Lord, come!*

For Discussion

1. Who do you think is the most powerful person in the world, and why?

2. How do you usually end your prayers? How would it change the flavor of your spiritual life to end your prayers with a word of praise?

3. Read the Old Testament equivalent of this doxology in 1 Chronicles 29:11. This is the prayer that David prayed when he was at the height of his kingly glory, after he had gathered all the materials to build the temple. How does knowing the context of this doxology enhance your understanding of the ending to the Lord's Prayer?

4. Contrast the prayer at the end of the Lord's Prayer, "Thine is the kingdom," with the one at the beginning, in which we pray for God's kingdom to come. What truths about the kingdom of God are expressed in the similarities and differences between these two phrases?

5. In order to better grasp God's power and glory, it's helpful to read Bible passages that give word pictures for the awesomeness of God, such as Psalm 47. In one sentence, what would you say is the theme of this psalm?

6. What types of power does the psalmist attribute to God in verses 2-5? (Complete the sentence: God has power over . . .)

7. What other things can you think of that God has power over? Think especially of what those who pray the Lord's Prayer trust God for.

8. What do you learn about God's glory from verses 5-9?

9. According to this psalm, what are some specific ways we should respond to God's power and glory? How can you respond to God's power and glory this week?

10. What word pictures, either from this psalm or from elsewhere in Scripture, help you to understand God's power and glory in a deeper way? For example, knowing that God is my powerful warrior (Ex. 15:3) reminds me that God has the power to save me from evil.

11. The Lord's Prayer ends on a victorious note. What truths from God's

Word help you remember that the victory is his? See Psalm 60 and 1 Corinthians 15:52-57 for some ideas.

12. What truth from the doxology at the end of the Lord's Prayer will you take away to help you in your prayer life this week?

13. Look back over the entire Lord's Prayer. What do these petitions say about the character of the God to whom we pray?

14. How has this study of the Lord's Prayer enriched your prayer life?

Notes

PREFACE

1. Adolph Saphir, quoted in Spiros Zodhiates, *The Lord's Prayer*, rev. edn. (Chattanooga, TN: AMG, 1991), 28-29.

CHAPTER 1:
HOW TO PRAY LIKE A HYPOCRITE

1. The painting is described but not identified in David M'Intyre, *The Hidden Life of Prayer* (Pensacola, FL: Chapel Library, n.d.), 3.

2. Augustine, "Our Lord's Sermon on the Mount," in *Saint Augustine: Sermon on the Mount, Harmony of the Gospels, Homilies on the Gospels*, ed. by Philip Schaff, Nicene and Post-Nicene Fathers, First Series, 14 vols. (Christian Literature, 1888; repr. Peabody, MA: Hendrickson, 1994), 6:1-63 (p. 37).

3. Spiros Zodhiates, *The Lord's Prayer*, rev. edn. (Chattanooga, TN: AMG, 1991), 5-6.

4. D. A. Carson, *Matthew*, Expositor's Bible Commentary, 12 vols. (Grand Rapids, MI: Zondervan, 1984), 8:165.

5. M'Intyre, 11.

6. M'Intyre, 11.

7. Samuel Lee, *Secret Prayer Successfully Managed*, in *The Puritans on Prayer*, ed. by Don Kistler (Morgan, PA: Soli Deo Gloria, 1995), 239-93 (p. 245).

8. Cyprian, "Treatise on the Lord's Prayer," in *Hippolytus, Cyprian, Caius, Novatian, Appendix*, ed. by Alexander Roberts and James Donaldson, Ante-Nicene Fathers, 10 vols. (Christian Literature, 1886; repr. Peabody, MA: Hendrickson, 1994), 5:447-57 (p. 448).

9. Andrew Murray, *With Christ in the School of Prayer* (Westwood, NJ: Fleming Revell, 1953), 30.

10. Zodhiates, 5.

11. John Paton, ed., *John G. Paton, DD, Missionary to the New Hebrides: An Autobiography*, 2 vols. (London, 1889) 1:10-11.

CHAPTER 2:
HOW TO PRAY LIKE AN ORPHAN

1. D. A. Carson, *Matthew*, Expositor's Bible Commentary, 12 vols. (Grand Rapids, MI: Zondervan, 1984), 8:165-66.

2. Martin Luther, "An Exposition of the Lord's Prayer for Simple Laymen, 1519," trans. by Martin H. Bertram, in *Devotional Writings I*, ed. by Martin O. Dietrich, *Luther's Works*, 55 vols. (Philadelphia: Fortress, 1969), 42:19.

3. Marshall Broomhall, *The Man Who Believed God: The Story of Hudson Taylor* (Chicago: Moody Press, 1929), 107-109.

CHAPTER 3:
HOW TO PRAY LIKE GOD'S OWN DEAR CHILD

1. Dietrich Bonhoeffer, *The Cost of Discipleship* (New York: Macmillan, 1969), 184.

2. Cyprian, "Treatise on the Lord's Prayer," in *Hippolytus, Cyprian, Caius, Novatian, Appendix*, ed. by Alexander Roberts and James Donaldson, Ante-Nicene Fathers, 10 vols. (Christian Literature, 1886; repr. Peabody, MA: Hendrickson, 1994), 5:447-57 (p. 449).

3. Ernst Lohmeyer, *"Our Father": An Introduction to the Lord's Prayer*, trans. by John Bowden (New York: Harper & Row, 1965), 14.

4. Elsie Anne McKee, "John Calvin's Teaching on the Lord's Prayer," in Daniel L. Migliore, ed., *The Lord's Prayer: Perspectives for Reclaiming Christian Prayer* (Grand Rapids, MI: Eerdmans, 1993), 88-106 (p. 94).

5. R. Kent Hughes, *Abba Father: The Lord's Pattern for Prayer* (Wheaton, IL: Crossway, 1986), 14.

6. The major positions are summarized in D. A. Carson, *Matthew*, Expositor's Bible Commentary, 12 vols. (Grand Rapids, MI: Zondervan, 1984), 8:167-68.

7. Tertullian, quoted in Brian J. Dodd, *Praying Jesus' Way: A Guide for Beginners and Veterans* (Downers Grove, IL: InterVarsity, 1997), 47.

8. Hugh Latimer, quoted in Spiros Zodhiates, *The Lord's Prayer*, rev. edn. (Chattanooga, TN: AMG, 1991), 28.

9. Zodhiates, vii.

10. Martin Luther, *The Table Talk of Martin Luther*, ed. by T. S. Kepler (New York: World Publishing, 1952), 209.

11. Zodhiates, 46.

12. The headings used to divide the Lord's Prayer come from the Reverend Dick Lucas, formerly of St. Helen Bishopsgate, London.

13. Cyprian, 5:449.

14. Cyprian, 5:448.

CHAPTER 4:
OUR FATHER IN HEAVEN

1. Kenneth L. Woodward, "Hallowed Be Thy Name," *Newsweek* (June 17, 1996), 75.

2. R. Kent Hughes, *Abba Father: The Lord's Pattern for Prayer* (Wheaton, IL: Crossway, 1986), 17-18.

3. See Herman Witsius, *Dissertations on the Lord's Prayer* (Edinburgh, 1839; repr. Escondido, CA: Den Dulk Christian Foundation, 1994), 146-52.

4. Leon Morris, *The Gospel According to Matthew* (Grand Rapids, MI: Eerdmans, 1992), 144.

5. Joachim Jeremias, *The Lord's Prayer*, trans. by John Reumann (Philadelphia: Fortress, 1964), 2.

6. Jeremias, 20.

7. David Blankenhorn, *Fatherless America: Confronting Our Most Urgent Social Problem* (New York: HarperCollins, 1995).

8. John G. Paton, *John G. Paton: Missionary to the New Hebrides* (Carlisle, PA: Banner of Truth, 1994).

9. John Shelby Spong, *Why Christianity Must Change or Die* (San Francisco: HarperCollins, 1998), 5.

10. James Barr, "Abba Isn't 'Daddy,'" *Journal of Theological Studies*, 39 (1988): 28-47.

11. Robert H. Gundry, *Matthew: A Commentary on His Handbook for a Mixed Church Under Persecution*, 2nd edn. (Grand Rapids, MI: Eerdmans, 1994), 105.

12. Herman N. Ridderbos, *Matthew*, trans. by Ray Togtman, Bible Student's Commentary (Grand Rapids, MI: Zondervan, 1987), 127.

13. J. I. Packer, *Knowing God* (Downers Grove, IL: InterVarsity, 1973), 182.

CHAPTER 5:
HOLY IS YOUR NAME

1. Timothy Bradshaw, *Praying as Believing: The Lord's Prayer and the Christian Doctrine of God*, Regent's Study Guides, 6 (Oxford: Regent's Park College, 1998), 51.

2. James Montgomery Boice, *Foundations of the Christian Faith*, rev. edn. (Downers Grove, IL: InterVarsity, 1986), 125.

3. William Shakespeare, *Romeo and Juliet*, II.ii.43-44.

4. Moses Maimonides, quoted in Spiros Zodhiates, *The Lord's Prayer*, rev. edn. (Chattanooga, TN: AMG, 1991), 118.

5. Augustine, "Our Lord's Sermon on the Mount," in *Saint Augustine: Sermon on the Mount, Harmony of the Gospels, Homilies on the Gospels*, ed. by Philip Schaff, Nicene and Post-Nicene Fathers, First Series, 14 vols. (Christian Literature, 1888; repr. Peabody, MA: Hendrickson, 1994), 6:1-63 (p. 40).

6. R. Kent Hughes, *Abba Father: The Lord's Pattern for Prayer* (Wheaton, IL: Crossway, 1986), 33.

7. Adapted from Zodhiates, 111.

8. Cyprian, "Treatise on the Lord's Prayer," in *Hippolytus, Cyprian, Caius, Novatian, Appendix*, ed. by Alexander Roberts and James Donaldson, Ante-Nicene Fathers, 10 vols. (Christian Literature, 1886; repr. Peabody, MA: Hendrickson, 1994), 5:447-57 (p. 450).

9. Martin Luther, *The Large Catechism* (Philadelphia: Fortress, 1959), 69.

10. Eric J. Alexander, "Plea for Revival," *tenth* (October, 1982), 24-32 (p. 30).

11. Thomas Watson, *The Lord's Prayer* (1692; repr. Edinburgh: Banner of Truth, 1960), 38.

CHAPTER 6:
YOUR KINGDOM COME

1. Helmut Thielicke, *Our Heavenly Father* (Grand Rapids, MI: Baker, 1980), 60, 62.

2. Ernst Lohmeyer, *"Our Father": An Introduction to the Lord's Prayer*, trans. by John Bowden (New York: Harper & Row, 1965), 100.

3. Spiros Zodhiates, *The Lord's Prayer*, rev. edn. (Chattanooga, TN: AMG, 1991), 141.

4. Martin Luther, "An Exposition of the Lord's Prayer for Simple Laymen, 1519," trans. by Martin H. Bertram, in *Devotional Writings I*, ed. by

Martin O. Dietrich, *Luther's Works*, 55 vols. (Philadelphia: Fortress, 1969), 42:37-38.

5. Richard Baxter, in Andrew F. Walls, "Old Athens and New Jerusalem: Some Signposts for Christian Scholarship in the Early History of Mission Studies," *International Bulletin of Missionary Research* (October, 1997), 146-53 (p. 146).

6. Darrell L. Guder, ed., *The Missional Church: A Vision for the Sending of the Church in North America* (Grand Rapids, MI: Eerdmans, 1998), 157.

7. Thomas Watson, *The Lord's Prayer* (1692; repr. Edinburgh: Banner of Truth, 1960), 59.

CHAPTER 7:
YOUR WILL BE DONE

1. John Calvin, *A Harmony of the Gospels: Matthew, Mark and Luke*, trans. by A. W. Morrison, ed. by D. W. Torrance and T. F. Torrance, 2 vols. (Grand Rapids, MI: Eerdmans, 1980), 2:206-207.

2. C. S. Lewis, *The Great Divorce* (New York: Macmillan, 1946), 72.

3. Darrell L. Guder, ed., *The Missional Church: A Vision for the Sending of the Church in North America* (Grand Rapids, MI: Eerdmans, 1998), 157-58.

4. Cyprian, "Treatise on the Lord's Prayer," in *Hippolytus, Cyprian, Caius, Novatian, Appendix*, ed. by Alexander Roberts and James Donaldson, Ante-Nicene Fathers, 10 vols. (Christian Literature, 1886; repr. Peabody, MA: Hendrickson, 1994), 5:447-57 (p. 451).

5. Martin Luther, "An Exposition of the Lord's Prayer for Simple Laymen, 1519," trans. by Martin H. Bertram, in *Devotional Writings I*, ed. by Martin O. Dietrich, *Luther's Works*, 55 vols. (Philadelphia: Fortress, 1969), 42:42.

6. Robert Coles, *The Spiritual Life of Children* (Boston: Houghton Mifflin, 1990), xiv.

7. Jean-Pierre de Caussade, *The Sacrament of the Present Moment*, trans. by Kitty Muggeridge (New York: Harper & Row, 1982), 75-76.

8. John Newton, quoted in D. Bruce Hindmarsh, *John Newton and the English Evangelical Tradition* (Oxford: Oxford University Press, 1996), 233.

9. Betty Scott Stam, quoted in Elisabeth Elliott, "Glorifying God in Mission," *Evangelicals Now* (November, 1998), 9.

10. *The Methodist Service Book* (London: Methodist Publishing House, 1975), D10.

CHAPTER 8:
GIVE US TODAY OUR DAILY BREAD

1. Origen, *Origen's Treatise on Prayer*, trans. and ed. by Eric George Jay (London: SPCK, 1954), 167.

2. Jerome, quoted in D. A. Carson, *Matthew*, Expositor's Bible Commentary, 12 vols. (Grand Rapids, MI: Zondervan, 1984), 8:171.

3. Tertullian, "On Prayer," *Latin Christianity: Its Founder, Tertullian, I, Apologetic; II. Anti-Marcion; III. Ethical*, trans. by S. Thelwall, ed. by Alexander Roberts and James Donaldson, Ante-Nicene Fathers, 10 vols. (1885; repr. Peabody, MA: Hendrickson, 1994), 3:683.

4. Don Brothy, "Why I Don't Pray Anymore," *National Catholic Reporter* (March 1, 1974), 9.

5. C. Stacey Woods, *Some Ways of God*, quoted in *Christianity Today* (September 7, 1998), 88.

6. Herman Witsius, *Dissertations on the Lord's Prayer* (Edinburgh, 1839; repr. Escondido, CA: Den Dulk Christian Foundation, 1994), 277.

7. William H. Willimon and Stanley Hauerwas, *Lord, Teach Us: The Lord's Prayer and the Christian Life* (Nashville, TN: Abingdon, 1996), 74.

8. Basil the Great, quoted in Willimon and Hauerwas, 76.

9. Origen, 171.

10. Donald A. Hagner, *Matthew 1-13*, Word Biblical Commentary (Dallas, TX: Word, 1993), 149.

11. Carson, 171.

12. Ernst Lohmeyer, *"Our Father": An Introduction to the Lord's Prayer*, trans. by John Bowden (New York: Harper & Row, 1965), 151.

13. Lohmyer, 140.

14. Brian J. Dodd, *Praying Jesus' Way: A Guide for Beginners and Veterans* (Downers Grove, IL: InterVarsity, 1997), 91, 128.

15. Hugo Grotius, quoted in Witsius, 282.

16. Gregory of Nyssa, quoted in Witsius, 295-96.

17. Hudson Taylor, in Marshall Broomhall, *The Man Who Believed God: The Story of Hudson Taylor* (Chicago: Moody, 1929), 150.

18. The story is told by H. A. Ironside in his *Illustrations of Bible Truth* (Chicago: Moody, 1945), 97-99, and recounted in James Montgomery Boice, *The Gospel of John: An Expositional Commentary* (Grand Rapids, MI: Zondervan, 1985), 774-75.

CHAPTER 9:
FORGIVE US OUR DEBTS

1. Herman Witsius, *Dissertations on the Lord's Prayer* (Edinburgh, 1839; repr. Escondido, CA: Den Dulk Christian Foundation, 1994), 315.

2. Witsius, 312.

3. Spiros Zodhiates, *The Lord's Prayer*, rev. edn. (Chattanooga, TN: AMG, 1991), 229.

4. David M'Intyre, *The Hidden Life of Prayer* (Pensacola, FL: Chapel Library, n.d.), 27.

CHAPTER 10:
AS WE FORGIVE OUR DEBTORS

1. Simon Wiesenthal, *The Sunflower: On the Possibilities and Limits of Forgiveness,* as reviewed by L. Gregory Jones in *Christianity Today* (October 26, 1998), 94-95.

2. Both Cyril and Augustine are discussed in Karlfried Froehlich, "The Lord's Prayer in Patristic Literature," in Daniel L. Migliore, ed., *The Lord's Prayer: Perspectives for Reclaiming Christian Prayer* (Grand Rapids, MI: Eerdmans, 1993), 71-87 (p. 85).

3. R. Kent Hughes, *Abba Father: The Lord's Pattern for Prayer* (Wheaton, IL: Crossway, 1986), 79.

4. Charles Haddon Spurgeon, *The Metropolitan Tabernacle Pulpit*, 63 vols. (Pasadena, TX: Pilgrim, 1969), 24:694.

5. Augustine, quoted in Hughes, 77.

6. William H. Willimon and Stanley Hauerwas, *Lord, Teach Us: The Lord's Prayer and the Christian Life* (Nashville, TN: Abingdon, 1996), 78.

7. Thomas Watson, *The Lord's Prayer* (1692; repr. Edinburgh: Banner of Truth, 1960), 214.

8. Augustine, quoted in Hughes, 80.

9. George Herbert, quoted in Willimon and Hauerwas, 83.

10. Brian J. Dodd, *Praying Jesus' Way: A Guide for Beginners and Veterans* (Downers Grove, IL: InterVarsity, 1997), 101.

11. Lewis Smedes, *Forgive and Forget* (San Francisco: Harper & Row, 1984), 94.

12. Richard Wurmbrand, "Give a Gem at Christmas," *The Voice of the Martyrs* (December, 1998), 14.

CHAPTER 11:
LEAD US NOT INTO TEMPTATION

1. Thomas Aquinas, quoted in Darrell L. Guder, ed., *Missional Church: A Vision for the Sending of the Church in North America* (Grand Rapids, MI: Eerdmans, 1998), 155.

2. Ernst Lohmeyer, *"Our Father": An Introduction to the Lord's Prayer,* trans. by John Bowden (New York: Harper & Row, 1965), 198.

3. Martin Luther, quoted in Thomas Watson, *The Lord's Prayer,* rev. edn. (London, 1692; repr. Edinburgh: Banner of Truth, 1965), 296.

4. Watson, 297.

5. Watson, 258.

6. Martin Luther, "An Exposition of the Lord's Prayer for Simple Laymen, 1519," trans. by Martin H. Bertram, in *Devotional Writings I,* ed. by Martin O. Dietrich, *Luther's Works,* 55 vols. (Philadelphia: Fortress, 1969), 42:71.

7. Reuters (February 13, 1998).

8. N. T. Wright, *The Lord and His Prayer* (Grand Rapids, MI: Eerdmans, 1996), 73.

9. Origen, *Origen's Treatise on Prayer,* trans. and ed. by Eric George Jay (London: SPCK, 1954), 190-91, 196.

10. b. Berakoth 60b (*The Babylonian Talmud*), quoted in Joachim Jeremias, *The Lord's Prayer,* trans. by John Reumann (Philadelphia: Fortress, 1964), 29.

11. Watson, 285.

12. Charles Haddon Spurgeon, *The Metropolitan Tabernacle Pulpit,* 63 vols. (Pasadena, TX: Pilgrim, 1969), 24:143, as retold by R. Kent Hughes in *Abba Father: The Lord's Pattern for Prayer* (Wheaton, IL: Crossway, 1986), 92-93.

CHAPTER 12:
DELIVER US FROM THE EVIL ONE

1. Herman Witsius, *Dissertations on the Lord's Prayer* (Edinburgh, 1839; repr. Escondido, CA: Den Dulk Christian Foundation, 1994), 362-63.

2. Martin Luther, "An Exposition of the Lord's Prayer for Simple Laymen, 1519," trans. by Martin H. Bertram, in *Devotional Writings I,* ed. by

Martin O. Dietrich, *Luther's Works*, 55 vols. (Philadelphia: Fortress, 1969), 42:75.

3. See D. A. Carson, *Matthew*, Expositor's Bible Commentary, 12 vols. (Grand Rapids, MI: Zondervan, 1984), 8:174.

4. Helmut Thielicke, *Our Heavenly Father* (Grand Rapids, MI: Baker, 1980), 133.

5. Witsius, 362.

6. C. S. Lewis, *The Screwtape Letters* (New York: Macmillan, 1962), 3.

7. Baudelaire, quoted in Donald Grey Barnhouse, *The Invisible War* (Grand Rapids, MI: Zondervan, 1965), 156.

8. Barnhouse, 103.

9. Witsius, 342-43.

10. John Calvin, *Institutes of the Christian Religion*, trans. by Ford Lewis Battles, 2 vols., Library of Christian Classics, 20-21 (Philadelphia, PA: Westminster, 1960), III.xx.46.

11. Spiros Zodhiates, *The Lord's Prayer*, rev. edn. (Chattanooga, TN: AMG, 1991), 295.

12. Thomas Watson, *The Lord's Prayer*, rev. edn. (London, 1692; repr. Edinburgh: Banner of Truth, 1965), 284.

13. Cyprian, "Treatise on the Lord's Prayer," in *Hippolytus, Cyprian, Caius, Novatian, Appendix*, ed. by Alexander Roberts and James Donaldson, Ante-Nicene Fathers, 10 vols. (Christian Literature, 1886; repr. Peabody, MA: Hendrickson, 1994), 5:447-57 (p. 455).

CHAPTER 13:
THE POWER AND THE GLORY

1. *The Didache (The Teaching of the Twelve Apostles)*, trans. by J. B. Lightfoot and J. R. Harmer, in *The Apostolic Fathers*, 2nd edn., ed. by Michael W. Holmes, (Grand Rapids, MI: Baker, 1989), 149-58 (p. 153).

2. Herman Witsius, *Dissertations on the Lord's Prayer* (Edinburgh, 1839; repr. Escondido, CA: Den Dulk Christian Foundation, 1994), 376.

3. Joachim Jeremias, *Unknown Sayings of Jesus* (London, 1958), 28.

4. Erasmus, quoted in Witsius, 370.

5. John Broadus, quoted in D. A. Carson, *Matthew*, Expositor's Bible Commentary, 12 vols. (Grand Rapids, MI: Zondervan, 1984), 8:174.

6. R. Kent Hughes, *Abba Father: The Lord's Pattern for Prayer* (Wheaton, IL: Crossway, 1986), 101.

7. Matthew Henry, *Commentary on the Whole Bible*, 6 vols. (New York: Revell, n.d.).

8. Arnaldo Momigliano, quoted in N. T. Wright, *The Lord and His Prayer* (Grand Rapids, MI: Eerdmans, 1996), 78.

9. Joachim Jeremias, *The Lord's Prayer*, trans. by John Reumann (Philadelphia: Fortress, 1964), 33.

10. Helmut Thielicke, *Our Heavenly Father* (Grand Rapids, MI: Baker, 1980), 77-78.

11. Jonathan Edwards, "The End for Which God Created the World," is reprinted in John Piper, *God's Passion for His Glory* (Wheaton, IL: Crossway, 1998), 125-251.

12. Edwards, 230.

13. Edwards, 233.

14. Jonathan Edwards, "Miscellany #3," in *The Miscellanies*, ed. by Thomas Schafer, *The Works of Jonathan Edwards* (New Haven, CT: Yale University Press, 1994), 13:199.

15. John Calvin, *Institutes of the Christian Religion*, trans. by Ford Lewis Battles, 2 vols., Library of Christian Classics, 20-21 (Philadelphia, PA: Westminster, 1960), III.xx.47.

16. Martin Luther, "An Exposition of the Lord's Prayer for Simple Laymen, 1519," trans. by Martin H. Bertram, in *Devotional Writings I*, ed. by Martin O. Dietrich, *Luther's Works*, 55 vols. (Philadelphia: Fortress, 1969), 42:76-7.

17. William H. Willimon and Stanley Hauerwas, *Lord, Teach Us: The Lord's Prayer and the Christian Life* (Nashville, TN: Abingdon, 1996), 108-109.

Index

Scripture Index